Flower Fingers:

Step-By-Step Flower Arranging

Flower Fingers
Step-By-Step
Flower Arranging

by Bernadette Wright

Photography by
Paul C. Wright S.D.A.D. (Phot.)

Consultant Editor Jim Mather
of the *Sunday Mirror*

W. Foulsham & Co. Ltd.
London · New York · Toronto ·
Cape Town · Sydney

FOR MY FAMILY

Appreciative thanks to Mollie Chitty of the
Guildford County College of Technology
without whose stimulating teaching this book
would never have been attempted.

My gratitude to my friend Doreen Phillips
who so generously allowed me limitless access
to her well stocked garden.

W. Foulsham & Company Limited,
Yeovil Road, Slough, Berkshire SL1 4JH

ISBN 0-572-01144-X
© Copyright W. Foulsham & Co. Ltd. 1982

Photoset in Great Britain by
Rowland Phototypesetting Ltd
Bury St Edmunds, Suffolk
Printed in Hong Kong

Contents

Introduction

Flowers have become very much a part of our everyday lives, and we eagerly welcome the first signs of their return after a long, cold winter. We use them as an expression of our feelings – as tokens of love and gratitude, and as a special gift to cheer the sick and the housebound.

Today, houseplants are to be found in many homes, merging harmoniously with the general decor. Fresh flowers, placed amongst them or arranged as a separate display, create extra life and colour, changing the whole atmosphere of a room. Flowers in the hall provide a special welcome, and can often become a talking point during the arrival of an unfamiliar guest.

Like any other craft, flower arranging has its 'do's and don'ts', but by following carefully a few simple rules, you will be surprised how quickly you will become skilled. Flower arranging for home decoration or as a hobby need not be expensive. It is very pleasant to own a few beautiful vases for your arrangements, but they are not absolutely necessary. Arrangements can be placed in concealed containers, plastic bowls, or any unusual or attractive receptacle that will hold water.

If you have to buy flowers, the choice is yours to spend as much or as little as you please. As you progress with the craft you will realize that there is much more to it than merely placing flowers in a vase. An attractive and pleasing design can be created from very ordinary materials at little or no cost. For instance, you can use twigs picked up after a storm, stones or moss with the addition of one or two flowers. A few twigs taken from a tree in your garden in spring will enhance your display by bursting into leaf. Flower arranging is a fascinating hobby, bringing new interests as we search for familiar materials to be used in different ways as part of the display. (For instance plastic or metal binding used in packaging can be formed into circles or other shapes as a support for twisted ivy.) The whole family becomes involved, and a walk in the country or a trip to the seaside becomes a treasure hunt for driftwood, bark, shells, dried grasses and seed heads, and the collection grows and grows as we see a possible future use in many familiar articles.

Join a flower-arranging club

I would recommend joining a flower-arranging club; you can usually go to a meeting as a visitor before making a decision to join. My introduction to flower arranging started in this way. On my first visit I was fortunate in seeing a first-class demonstration using the most colourful exotic flowers – I was entranced. I enjoyed the monthly meetings for a whole year before I had the courage to join a beginners' class, where I found interest, friendship and relaxation. At meetings most clubs provide a sales table where essential pieces of equipment can be purchased at reasonable prices. Members may also bring surplus garden plants to be sold cheaply in aid of club funds – a wonderful way to stock your garden. Competitive arranging appeals to many: it is a wide-ranging subject requiring extra study, and includes the making of pictures, swags, ornamental wreaths, collages, garlands, etc. The work must conform to a set of rules, but it is all very light-hearted and enjoyable. There are also non-competitive exhibitions to take part in, such as flower festivals in churches and cathedrals.

The flower arranging clubs as a whole raise many thousands of pounds annually for charity. It is a great source of satisfaction to members that they can combine personal enjoyment with much needed help to others. Most clubs are affiliated to the National Association of Flower Arrangement Societies of Great Britain, known as (NAFAS).

This book has been compiled as a working manual with the busy and inexperienced in mind, to help to change what might be thought of as just another part of housework into an enjoyable and relaxing pursuit. Whether your flowers are a planned purchase, bought on impulse, or received as a gift, by following the step-by-step instructions included here, you should achieve a successful and long-lasting arrangement that will not only give you personal satisfaction, but also bring pleasure to your family and friends.

Equipment

General equipment

Flower arranging requires a few basic but essential pieces of equipment. The following list covers general articles that you will need to use whenever you want to arrange fresh flowers or foliage.

1. A strong pair of sharp scissors or secateurs. Special flower scissors, although not essential, are a good buy. They have a serrated blade that makes cutting stems much easier. A notch at the base of the blade is useful for cutting wire.
2. A deep bucket to hold flowers and foliage whilst you work out your arrangement.
3. A polythene sheet to cover your work surface and to reduce the task of cleaning up.
4. A watering can or teapot to top up your finished arrangement.
5. A watering spray is useful to freshen up the arrangement from time to time.
6. A small sharp knife.

Mechanics

This is a collective term used to describe the devices that hold the stems in position. They may be specially designed pieces of equipment that are easily obtainable at florists, supermarkets, or hardware stores, or they may be ordinary household materials adapted to suit your purposes.

Wire netting
Cheap-grade chicken wire with a wide mesh can be folded easily to fit into a deep container. Avoid the plastic-coated variety, which is not as pliable, and is difficult to use.

Equipment

watering spray

watering can

roll of polythene

flower scissors

deep bucket

Pinholders

Pinholders have a heavy, flat lead base covered by closely packed, sharp rustless pins about 2 to 3.5 cm (1 to 1½ in) long. They vary in size and shape. A round one 6 to 8 cm (2½ to 3 in) in diameter is a good general size and most useful for a quick and simple arrangement. It is a good investment and will serve you well for many years – some of mine are 15 years old and still in use. Beware of false economy: the plastic varieties with suction pads are not usually so effective. They are not heavy enough to give the stable foundation necessary to a good flower arrangement.

Well pinholder

This is a pinholder that is incorporated into its own lead container. An ordinary pinholder placed in a food tin and secured by strong glue or plasticine serves the same purpose but is not as heavy and does not provide as good a base.

Candlecups

These are small containers made to fit into the top of a candlestick, bottle, or similar narrow-mouthed container.

Foam saucer

A foam saucer is an inexpensive plastic dish into which a round of plastic foam fits snugly.

Foam anchors

Foam anchors are available in either metal or plastic, and can be used with either wet or dry foam. The plastic variety costs only a few pence. It is a good idea to have anchors fixed permanently with strong glue in the containers that will be used quite frequently.

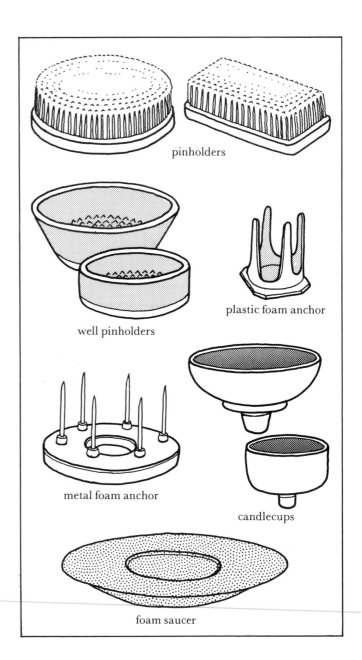

pinholders

well pinholders

plastic foam anchor

metal foam anchor

candlecups

foam saucer

Plastic foam

Plastic foam is a water-absorbent substance sold under various trade names, such as 'Oasis' and 'Florapack'. It can be bought in a number of shapes and sizes. The rounds and squares are usually large enough for normal-sized home decorations and can be cut into smaller pieces with a sharp knife if required.

Dry plastic foam

Dry plastic foam, sold under trade names such as Styrofoam and Drihold, is for use with preserved plant material. It comes in the same shapes and sizes as the water-retaining kind.

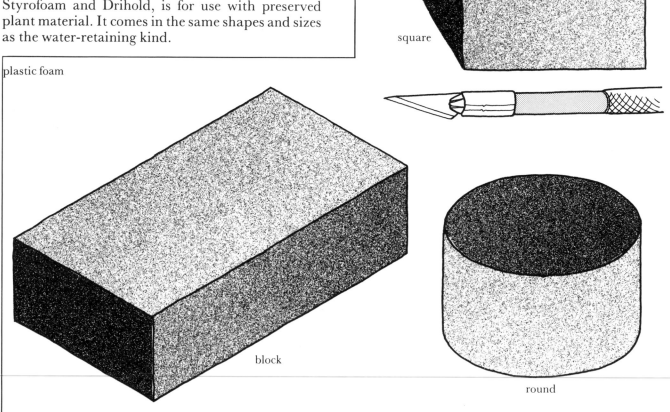

plastic foam

square

block

round

Jugs, jars and other containers

Attractive jugs and jars make useful containers since they can hold a large amount of water. The best way to use a jug is to fill it with chicken wire. Use wire as wide as the jug, and three times its height. Fold it into a U-shape and push it down into the container with the cut ends uppermost. The cut ends can be wrapped around stems to hold them securely in position. This method can also be used for a straight-sided container.

Large wide-mouthed and straight-sided containers can be loosely filled with woody twigs from which all the leaves have been removed. The twigs are cut off level with the top of the container and the stems are inserted between the twigs, which hold them in position.

wire netting in a U-shape

jug with wire netting
4–5 cm (1½–2 in) gauge

cut ends
upwards

straight-sided jar
filled with twigs

A bottle or narrow-necked vase that holds only one or two stems can be wedged with a short extra piece of stem hidden by a leaf. A wedge of newspaper or tissue could be used instead.

For smaller dainty flowers, a vase criss-crossed over the top with adhesive tape is the answer. The spaces can be made quite small for the finest stems. It is essential to make sure that the container is quite dry, otherwise the tape will not adhere to the vase and the arrangement will collapse.

A shallow dish or cereal bowl can be used to hold a flower arrangement by gluing a pinholder to the bottom and pushing wire netting onto it. Alternatively, folded wire netting can be held in place with rubber bands.

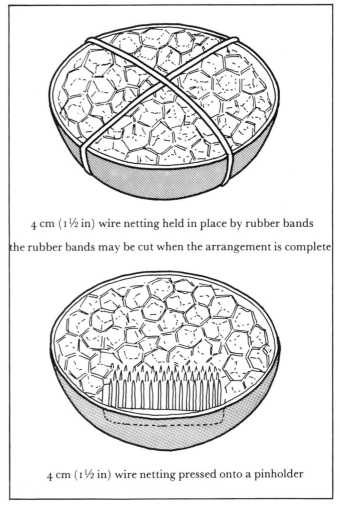

4 cm (1½ in) wire netting held in place by rubber bands

the rubber bands may be cut when the arrangement is complete

4 cm (1½ in) wire netting pressed onto a pinholder

criss-crossed adhesive tape covering top of container

If you have only a few flowers and a large container it is a good idea to arrange the flowers in a smaller vessel placed inside the larger one.

Articles to collect

Collect bottles and food tins of different shapes and sizes and paint them or cover with fabrics of different textures and designs. A shallow, narrow rectangular tin is useful for a horizontal design or for a crescent-shaped arrangement.

Oddments of various fabrics should be kept to cover bases, and it is a good idea to keep pieces of wood, stone and slate that can be used as bases or accessories in landscape designs.

Broken windscreen glass is useful for covering a pinholder in a water arrangement and small pebbles of different colours can be used to cover mechanics.

All kinds of driftwood should be stored, even small pieces, which can be built up into a more interesting shape. Twisted branches, bark, cones, feathers, leathery leaves, seashells and numerous items that can be picked up on excursions out-of-doors should always be kept. There will sometimes be an occasion when one of these odd bits and pieces will be just the thing to put the finishing touch to your arrangement.

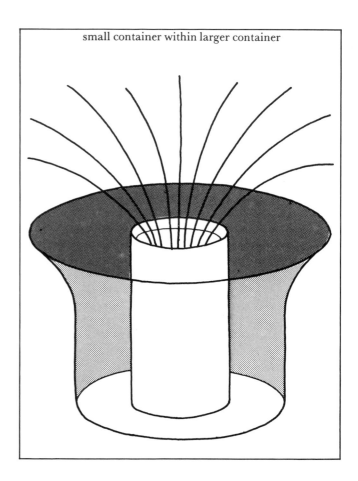
small container within larger container

Preparing plant material for use

Fresh and preserved foliage, flowers, berries, seed-heads, fruit, vegetables, and driftwood are all referred to as plant material by flower arrangers. Any fresh plant material must be *conditioned* before you begin your arrangement.

Conditioning is the term used to describe the care and preparation given to fresh plant material to promote longer life after it has been cut, making sure that it is able to absorb water. Conditioning begins as soon as plants are cut from the garden, or as soon as they are obtained from the florist. Instructions for conditioning the various fresh materials available are given below.

Fresh plant material

Flowers from the florist or nursery
If possible flowers should be bought at different stages of development so that there is a variety of flower size. For example, when you buy spray chrysanthemums (those with more than one flower on each stem) some will be in full flower and some still in bud. Accept only fresh flowers – they will last longer and give more pleasure. The following hints should help you to distinguish between the freshest of flowers and those that have been in the shop for some time: yellow-centred flowers become darker as they get older; carnations should feel papery; and in general, foliage on the flowers should be crisp and bright in colour, and the stems should be firm and not feel slimy or look discoloured.

The stem ends of cut flowers that have been out of water for a time become dry and seal over. To condition them re-cut as soon as possible, removing about 2.5 cm (1 in), and place the stem ends in warm water. Leave for two hours or overnight to help the flowers revive before using them in an arrangement.

Cut flowers from the garden
Take a bucket half-filled with tepid water with you and place the flowers in it as soon as they are cut so that the stem ends do not seal over. If you do this, further conditioning will not be necessary. Leave the flowers in a cool room for at least two hours, or overnight, before arranging. Never cut flowers in bright sunshine; they become dehydrated and limp in the heat. Always gather your material in the cool of the day, either morning or evening, when it is at its best.

Foliage
Foliage benefits from being submerged completely in warm water for at least two hours before use. Hard, glossy and mature foliage may be left submerged overnight. Submersion washes the leaves clean and charges the foliage with water so that it will stay fresh and green longer.

Grey foliage is an exceptional case. The grey surface of the leaves is due to a covering of fine grey hairs and, if submerged, these will become waterlogged and look very sad and bedraggled. The soggy leaves may drip and spoil furniture. The stem ends only should be placed in water for a little while before arranging.

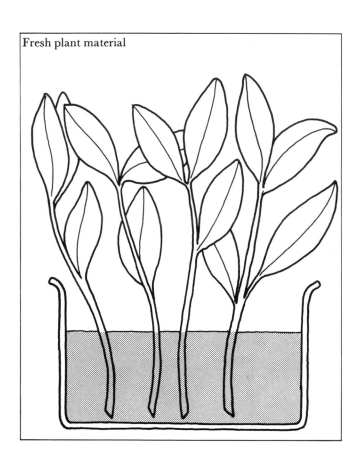

Fresh plant material

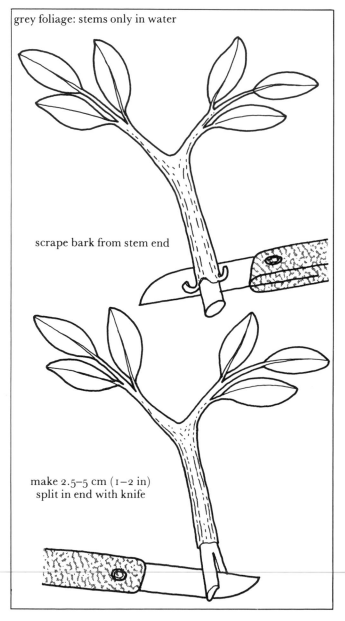

grey foliage: stems only in water

scrape bark from stem end

make 2.5–5 cm (1–2 in) split in end with knife

Stems

Plants vary quite considerably in their stem structures and different types of stem require very different conditioning.

Hard and woody stems Remove the lower leaves and scrape off about 5 cm (2 in) of bark. Split the ends with a sharp knife, so that the plant is able to absorb water more easily. Place in hand-warm water.

Milky stems The stems of plants such as spurges and poppies exude a milky substance, which dries and blocks the stem ends, preventing water from being drawn up to the flower head. Burn the ends with a match or lighter for a few seconds and place in deep, warm water.

Soft stems Spring flowers such as daffodils have soft stems. Cut about 3 cm (just over an inch), or the white part, off the ends and stand in tepid water until ready to use.

Hollow stems Delphiniums and lupins are examples of hollow-stemmed flowers. Turn them upside down and, using a funnel or a fine-spouted watering can, fill the stem with warm water. Plug the end with tissue or hold a finger over the end while replacing under water in a deep bucket. A flower bucket is the best type to use. I have never found this treatment necessary for delphiniums, but lupins can benefit from this conditioning. If this fails and the lupin droops, 'boil' as described in First aid treatment overleaf.

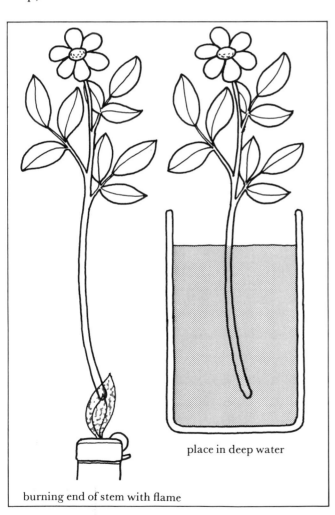

place in deep water

burning end of stem with flame

filling hollow stem

First aid treatment
If flowers or foliage wilt they can usually be revived. Remove from the arrangement. Cut off about 3 cm (just over an inch) of stem and stand or float in warm water for two hours or until recovered.

'Boiling' is a more drastic form of first aid treat-ment. This is employed for removing an air lock which may have formed when the stem was cut, thus preventing water reaching the flower. It may sound a rather harsh treatment for flowers, but the results are excellent. Re-cut and hold the stems in the hand, covering the foliage and blooms with a cloth. Plunge the stem ends into 3 cm (just over an inch) or so of boiling water in a saucepan for half a minute. This drives out the air lock and allows the stem to take up water again. Transfer water and stems to another container. Add some more warm water and leave until the plant material revives. This treatment is particularly effective with florists' roses, which sometimes hang their heads. Before plunging the ends in the boiling water, straighten the heads carefully and roll each one separately in newspaper. This keeps the bloom upright while the stem is absorbing water. Leave wrapped until the stem revives.

Grooming
When beginning an arrangement, remove all the lower leaves that might be under water and may decompose. Prune out any damaged leaves and any that are growing too closely together and which might spoil the shape. Leaves with damaged edges may be trimmed into shape with scissors. This will not shorten their life or harm them in any way. The thorns of roses, berberis, etc., should be removed for ease in arranging and to prevent damage to fingers and other plant material.

Preserved plant material

A store of preserved plant material is most useful in winter when fresh foliage and flowers are scarce. It can be mixed with fresh plant material or used alone. It is particularly suitable for use in centrally

floating leaves and flowers in warm water

protect leaves and flowers from steam by covering with a cloth

wrapping a rose in newspaper

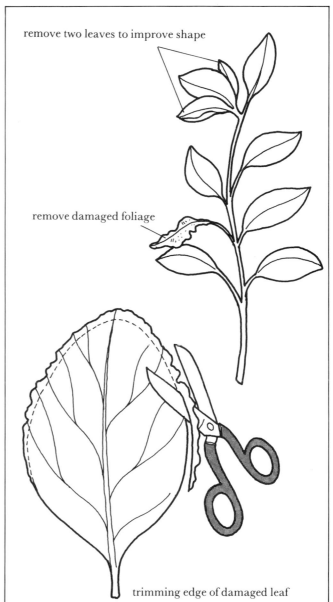

remove two leaves to improve shape

remove damaged foliage

trimming edge of damaged leaf

heated buildings in which fresh arrangements have a short life and is a boon to flat-dwellers, providing them with a long-lasting decoration that can be varied by the addition of fresh flowers when they are available. Preserved material provides foliage of different colours, for example, *Choisya*, box, and *Aspidistra* treated with glycerine are a beautiful cream colour, while most other foliages turn varying shades of brown.

Three methods of preserving plant material are described in detail below. It is well worth taking time and trouble over the treatment, for once preserved the flowers and foliage can be used again and again and will last you a very long time.

The glycerine method

July is a good month to begin treatment, for many plants are at their best at this time – mature but not too old. If they are treated too early they will not absorb the solution.

Select attractively shaped branches. Prune out any damaged leaves and those that spoil the shape of the stem. Scrape off a few centimetres of bark from the stem end and split the end with a sharp knife as described on page 18. Condition in warm water for an hour or so. The material is now ready for treatment. To make up the solution take one part glycerine and two parts of very hot (just off boiling) water and mix them well in a jar. Place the stem ends in the warm glycerine-and-water solution – up to about 5 cm (2 in) depth is usually enough. Keep in a dry room until all the leaves have changed colour and feel pliable. The time taken varies according to the type of material. Most foliages, such as beech, take about three days. Plants with heavier tissue, such as *Aspidistra*, absorb the solution more slowly and their leaves benefit from being wiped over on

both sides with the glycerine-and-water mixture. It may be three weeks or longer before they are ready. If all the solution is absorbed before the plants are ready, just add a little more.

When the leaves are ready, remove them from the solution. Wrap the stem ends in tissue so that they do not drip. Tie them in small bunches and hang on a

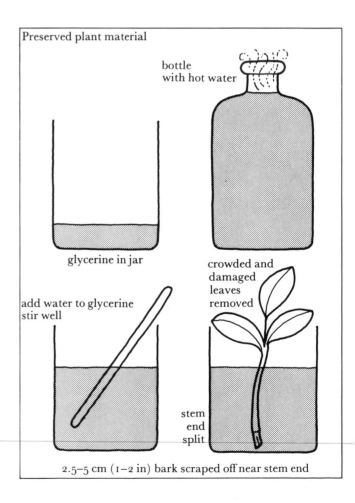

Preserved plant material

bottle with hot water

glycerine in jar

add water to glycerine stir well

crowded and damaged leaves removed

stem end split

2.5–5 cm (1–2 in) bark scraped off near stem end

clothes horse or a coat hanger depending on the quantity. If you wish, they can now be moved out-of-doors to bleach in the sun.

When treatment is complete the material should be stored in a cardboard box in a dry place. If the leaves look crushed when you wish to use them, hold them in the steam of a kettle for a few seconds and they will be restored. The glycerine solution can be re-heated and used again. Try experimenting at intervals during the summer; you will find that there is a difference in colouring as the plants grow older. Autumn is too late to begin; the sap is returning to the roots and the leaves are beginning to fall.

Pressing
Pressing is not a suitable method of preserving foliage to be used in an arrangement as it becomes too brittle and damages easily. It is also rather flat in appearance.

Air drying
Air drying is a very simple method of preservation and is suitable for many types of plant material. There are a number of suitable annuals that can be grown from seed, for example *Acroclinium*, *Statice*, *Rhodanthe*, and *Helichrysum*. The stems of *Helichrysum* (everlasting flowers) are very bulky. It is a good idea to cut them off (about 1 cm from the flower head) as soon as the flowers are picked, and to replace them with a false stem. Insert a rose wire (available from florists or garden centres) through the stem into the head of the flower. This will contract as it dries and so hold the wire securely.

Other plants suitable for air drying are *Anaphilis*, *Achillea*, delphiniums and lavender. These should be gathered on a dry day before they are in full flower, with some buds just showing colour, and with some open blooms. Tie them in small bundles and hang them upside down in a dark dry cupboard. A wire coat hanger makes a convenient rail. They will be dry and ready to use in a few days.

There is a wealth of material to be found growing in the countryside. The many varieties of grasses

glycerined material ready to place in sunshine to bleach
(stem ends wrapped in tissue)

should be picked early in the year, before they are fully mature and begin to shed their seeds. Pussy willow must be gathered when the soft, silky white buds appear, and reedmace (bullrush) in June, before it is fully mature. When dry these plants should be sprayed with hair lacquer to prevent them bursting open and dropping seeds later in the year. After spraying hang them to dry again. All the plants mentioned above will take much longer to dry out completely than the self-drying annuals.

Seed-heads look very attractive in arrangements of dry material, providing a variety of forms and colours. Plants with suitable seed-heads include *Allium*, *Clematis*, love-in-a-mist, poppy, chinese lantern, dock, honesty, pampas grass, and teasel. These dry well if left in the garden and should be picked when the heads change colour, before they are spoiled by the weather. They can be tied together in bundles and hung upside down to finish drying in the same way as the grasses.

flower head with
1 cm (½ in) stem

flower head with
rose wire inserted

as flower head shrinks,
cut off wire if it becomes
visible

using rose wire ensures
that the flower will not
be discoloured by rust

before using in an arrangement,
strengthen the stem
place a 22 gauge stub wire alongside the
rose wire and bend together with florists'
tape or 0.5 cm (¼ in) strip of crepe paper

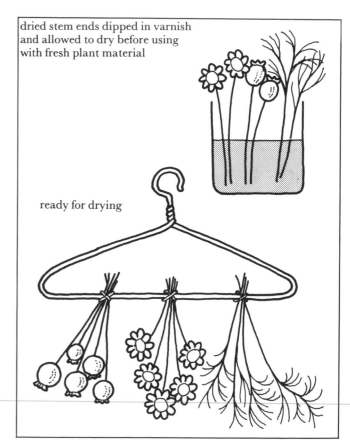

dried stem ends dipped in varnish
and allowed to dry before using
with fresh plant material

ready for drying

Drying in shallow water
The seed-heads of hydrangeas develop a papery texture in the autumn. When they have reached this stage pick them and stand in shallow water, about 3 cm (just over an inch) deep, and leave until all the water has dried up. I obtain good results by putting the hydrangea stems in an old piece of damp plastic foam in a warm place and allowing the foam and flowers to dry out. This takes about three weeks.

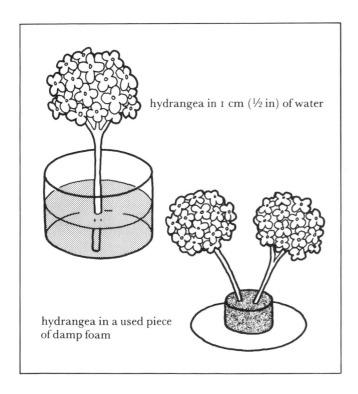

hydrangea in 1 cm (½ in) of water

hydrangea in a used piece of damp foam

Before storing naturally dried material dip the stems into polyurethane varnish for a few seconds and allow them to dry. This prevents them absorb-

ing water when used in an arrangement with fresh material.

Preserving fruit and vegetables
Gourds come in many shapes and sizes and are well worth drying. They are easy to grow from seed, or are sometimes available from florists. Artichokes, oranges, lemons, and pomegranates can also be dried. Any fruit and vegetables that you want to dry should be placed in an open box in the airing cupboard. Artichokes dry in about a week; the others take longer. You can judge when they are ready by their weight: they will feel light and empty, and hard to the touch. They may be painted to use in festive decorations. Gourds look more attractive with a coat of varnish, which deepens their colours and helps to preserve them.

Driftwood

Driftwood is the term used to describe weathered wood of all descriptions, not just the oddly shaped bleached branches collected from the seashore. It can range from the leafless stems of ivy, honeysuckle, or wisteria to slices from tree trunks, roots, or bark. Small chunky pieces are useful for hiding mechanics, and look well in the landscape type of design. In winter, when flowers are scarce, an attractive design can be achieved by the inclusion of the more shapely pieces with very few flowers. Driftwood, already cleaned and prepared, can be purchased from garden centres and florists but it is more exciting and satisfying to build up a personal collection of pieces found on excursions to the seashore or the countryside. A walk in the woods or by a river after a storm can be rewarding in this respect.

To clean the driftwood you have collected, soak it overnight in water with detergent added, to remove dirt and any insects. Scrub well and allow to dry. Brush well using a wire brush and, with a small knife, dig out the soft parts. Finish by polishing with a colourless wax, which will improve the appearance and help to preserve the wood.

To lighten dark wood after cleaning, soak in a mixture of water and bleach (one part bleach to eight parts water) for about a week. Rinse off with clean water and leave outside to dry.

When using driftwood in an arrangement, the heavier pieces can often stand alone. If they are uneven, a little piece can be sawn from the bottom, or it can be propped up with a chunky piece of wood. Thinner pieces can be impaled on a pinholder or inserted into plastic foam. They can also be placed on top of, or over the edge of, a container.

Driftwood

wire brush for cleaning

pointed knife for cleaning out cavities

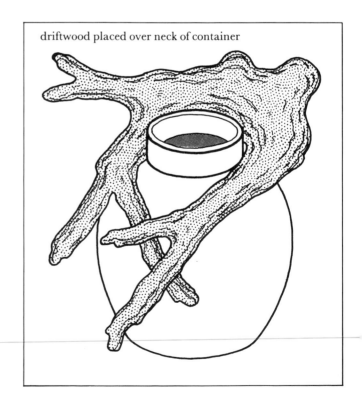

driftwood placed over neck of container

Making a start

Have everything to hand – plant material, container, mechanics and the other accessories described earlier – and cover the work surface with a plastic sheet or newspaper. If the flowers are to be arranged for a special occasion, arrange them the day before; you will then have one less job to do on the day. Sit down to work. If you are making a table arrangement, it is essential to sit down in order to have the same view of the arrangement as your guests. Relax and enjoy working with beautiful materials. If things are going badly – leave it for a while, have a cup of coffee and when you return you will be surprised at how quickly things will go your way.

Before commencing an arrangement there are a number of points to be considered.

What size and shape?

The size and shape of your arrangement will depend on the amount of space available. A small amount of space calls for a small arrangement or, if there is little width available, for a tall sparse one. Do not try to crowd a large arrangement into a cramped space. If you are in doubt, the empty container placed in the intended position is a good guide. Re-arrange any ornaments that might intrude to spoil the finished design.

Choosing a style

A flower design with a lot of plant material is described as a 'mass' or 'traditional' arrangement. A 'modern' or 'free-form' design has a minimum of plant material. Both forms have to *be* balanced as well as looking balanced. A traditional arrangement must look as if it radiates from the centre, where the largest and most beautiful flower is placed, forming the 'point of interest'.

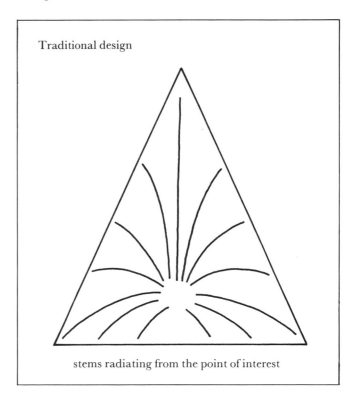

Traditional design

stems radiating from the point of interest

For a modern or free-form design it is not necessary to have the point of interest in the centre, but when looked at with half-closed eyes, it must balance on both sides of an imaginary line through the centre of the arrangement.

A traditional design should always have a recognizable shape. To obtain this, it is first necessary to make a good outline using narrow foliage. The larger flowers are used to create an area of interest in the centre from which all the stems appear to radiate. The centre and the outline are joined with graduated 'transitional' shapes, the leaves and flowers becoming larger towards the centre.

In traditional arrangements, generally the first placement of outline material defines the height of the arrangement. It should be at least one-and-a-half times the largest dimension of the container. If the

Modern design

more than one
point of interest

two flowers of equal size, and two leaves balanced either side of long, central leaf

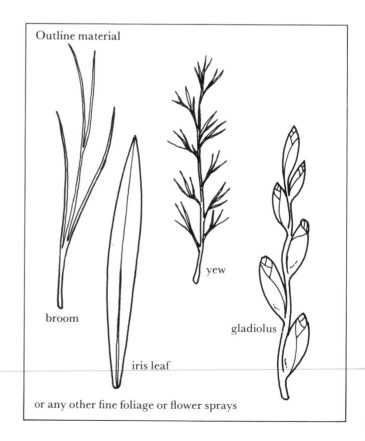

Outline material

broom

iris leaf

yew

gladiolus

or any other fine foliage or flower sprays

height of the container is greater than the width, then the first stem should be one-and-a-half times the height: for example, if the container is 20 cm (8 in) high, add 10 cm (4 in) to give 30 cm (12 in). Allow for the height of the foam and cut the stem about 35 cm (14 in) long. If the width is the greater then the first stem will be one-and-a-half times the width of the container. A 'vertical' design can be taller – two or three times the largest dimension of the container. The different styles of arrangement are discussed in more detail on pages 37–56.

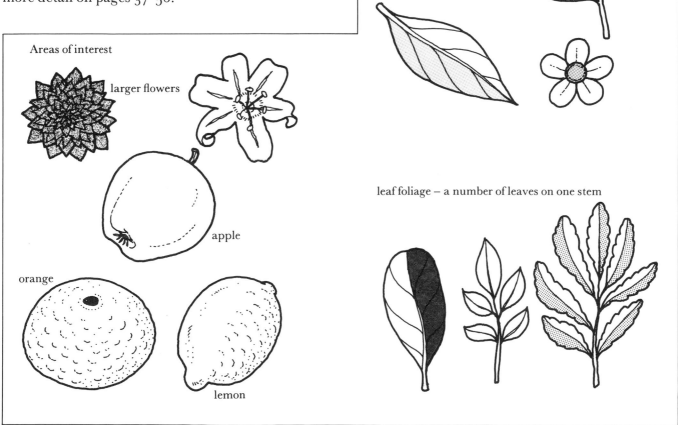

Transitional shapes

Areas of interest

larger flowers

apple

orange

lemon

leaf foliage – a number of leaves on one stem

Choosing colours

Colour is the most eye-catching element in a design. It can be harmonious – as in mass arrangements, or spectacular – as in the more modern designs. Choosing the right colour combinations to complement each other is not always easy, but it comes with practice. After all, we choose everything in our homes – furnishings, tableware, linen and kitchen utensils. In nature there is colour everywhere – in the flowers, vegetables, fruit, stones and wood, and all the colours are blended in harmony by many shades of green.

Your flowers can be used to convey a particular atmosphere. For *harmony* choose flowers of a colour in keeping with the general decor of the room; for example pick a colour from your curtains. A *dark corner* can be lightened by the use of pale colours – white, yellow or pale pink, with light green foliage. A more lively note can be achieved by the introduction of brighter contrasting colours, such as orange with blue, yellow with purple, or red with green or blue. Red and orange give an impression of warmth and is a good combination for cold north-facing rooms. Blue and mauve are absorbed into the background. They need bright light to show them to advantage, and so are not suitable for candlelit occasions. On a hot day, a foliage arrangement of greens and greys looks cool and refreshing and can also add brightness to a cheerless winter day. For *table arrangements*, flowers can be chosen to match the china, tablecloth, candles, candlesticks or napkins. Do not use highly perfumed flowers which may mar the aroma of the food to be served.

Impulse buying, or flowers received as a gift, may cause problems, since they may be difficult to match to the general decor. The answer is to create for them a special area. The arrangement on page 78 demonstrates this situation. The roses, although beautiful in themselves, lacked interest. When placed next to the shiny blue cat, however, the contrast gave them vitality and impact. The cat would be too dominant for the show bench, but here we are dealing with flowers to enjoy in the home.

Balance

All arrangements should have *actual balance*. This means that they should be stable, without the possibility of falling over. Generally designs are viewed from the front, so we naturally put our best flowers and foliage there. Be practical, however, and put equal weight to the back. Less beautiful and shorter pieces of foliage and leaves are suitable as they will be unseen.

Visual balance
Visual balance is equally important. In a traditional arrangement, although it may be stable, a large dark flower or a brilliant one near the top, will give an unbalanced look. The point of interest is in the centre, near the base, which is where the prominent blooms should be. If you are in doubt, hold a ruler in the centre of the arrangement and view with half-closed eyes. Balance in a free-form design, with more than one point of interest, is equally important.

Size (scale)
The size of the flowers is important. They should be in keeping with the size of the container, and should also relate to the setting where they are to be placed. Spray chrysanthemums and flowers of similar size are large enough for a table decoration. Single daisy-like varieties look lighter. Large heavy blooms need a

large container, and are suitable for display in a large room. Small delicate flowers require a small dainty container. Experiment with different sizes and you will soon discover that components closely related in scale give a more balanced design.

Form (shapes)
Variation of shape prevents dullness. Take, for instance, a bunch of carnations or chrysanthemums. To arrange these round flowers with round leaves would be boring. Include fine outline material and pointed leaves. Turn some of the flower heads sideways and interest is created. Flowers of different shapes arranged together will also provoke much interest.

Texture

All plant material has textural qualities. The following list indicates these qualities.

Shiny	Camellia foliage, laurel.
Smooth	Bergenia, periwinkle, privet.
Fluffy	Pampas grass, clematis seed heads.
Rough	Bark, heather, fir cones.
Prickly	Teasel, sea holly.
Velvety	Pussy willow, pansy, wallflowers, *Stachys lanata* leaves, peaches.
Sticky	Horse chestnut buds.
Crisp	Bracken, iris leaves.
Waxy	Water lily, camellia flowers, Anthurium blooms.
Dull	Grey foliage, fungi.
Thorny	Gorse, rose stems, berberis.

Contrasting textures enhance each other; place a shiny surface next to a matt surface. Texture may also be introduced by any other of the components in the design, such as the base, accessory or container.

A small amount of a shiny texture balances a much larger amount of dull material. Contrasting textures, used with restraint, give extra lift to an arrangement. To the inexperienced, my advice is to concentrate on achieving good shapes with suitable foliage and flowers, and then later, with confidence, experiment with these other elements.

Choosing the container

Containers, if they are visible, should be in keeping with the style of the arrangement. In an harmonious design, they should not detract from the arrangement by being highly coloured or too shiny. In modern arrangements they can be more eye-catching and can play a part in your design, but the plant material must always dominate the overall design. Flowers look more attractive in a raised container. When using a basket or a foam saucer, it is a good idea to raise it slightly for a better effect, by placing it on a slice of wood, empty food tin, cheese board, or other suitable base. A raised container is a must for some designs; for instance The Hogarth Curve and the Inverted Crescent.

Containers need not be expensive – a good shape is more important than any other feature. My favourite container is a scratched glass cake dish on an aluminium base, which I bought at a jumble sale. It has been painted many colours: at the moment it is black. Roses of all colours, marigolds and daisy-like flowers look especially attractive arranged in it.

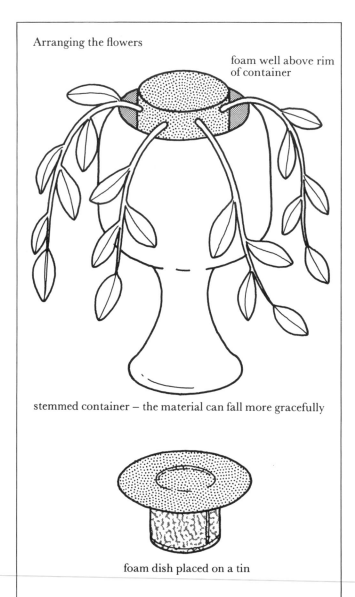

Arranging the flowers

foam well above rim of container

stemmed container – the material can fall more gracefully

foam dish placed on a tin

Choosing the base

Anything on which the container is placed is called a base. Bases are useful for a number of reasons:

1. To protect furniture from water staining and scratching. Unglazed pottery sweats and leaves an ugly stain that is difficult to remove.

2. To enhance the colour in an arrangement, for example, the base can be covered with fabric of the same colour as the flowers, giving a richer colour to the design.

3. Many arrangements can be placed in a well pinholder, without the need for a container, if they are placed on a base of wood, slate, stone, glass or similar. Table mats of cork, bamboo straw or similar materials are also useful.

4. If the container looks too small for the arrangement, the use of a base can counteract this.

A fabric-covered base is easy to make. It can be a cake board, a small tray, or a cardboard plate; in fact it can be anything of the required shape. To cover a base, place the board or tray on the reverse side of the fabric. Draw around it and cut out, allowing about 5 cm (2 in) extra for a hem. Make the hem about 2.5 cm (1 in) wide and leave an opening into which a piece of thin elastic can be threaded. Thread the elastic through and pull it tight until it fits the base snugly, and then tie a knot in it. A number of covers can be made from different coloured fabrics to fit one base so that when you want to use a different base all you have to do is pull off one cover and replace it with another.

To make an oval base I draw around an oval meat dish and cut the base from a thick cardboard box.

Making the base

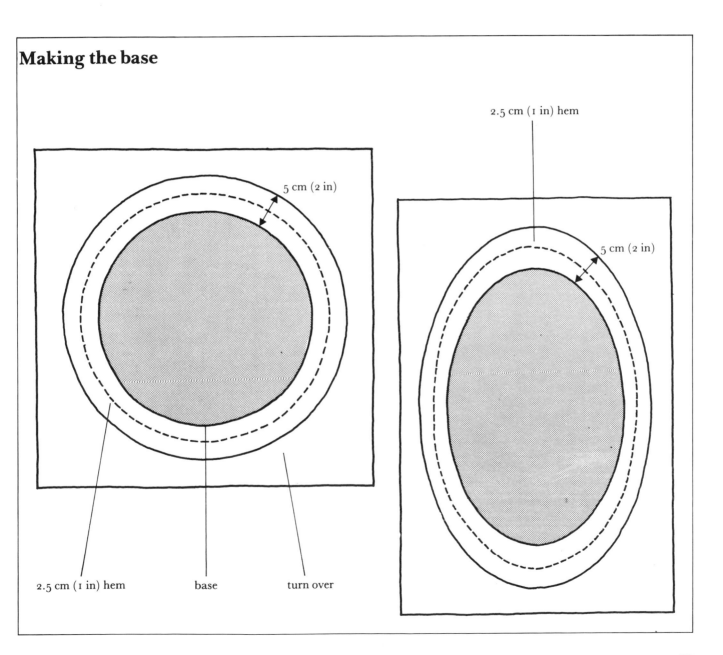

5 cm (2 in)

2.5 cm (1 in) hem   base   turn over

2.5 cm (1 in) hem

5 cm (2 in)

Measurement of arrangements

The size of the container determines the dimension of the arrangement. Generally, the first placement of outline material defines the height of the arrangement. It should be at least one-and-a-half times the largest dimension of the container. If the height of the container is greater than the width, then the first stem should be one-and-a-half times the height, for instance, if the container is 20 cm (8 in) high, then it should be + 10 cm (4 in) = 30 cm (12 in). Allow for the foam by cutting the stem 33–35 cm (13–14 in) long. If the width is the greater, then the first stem will be one-and-a-half times the width.

A *vertical* design can be taller – twice or more the largest dimension of the container. When using a hidden container on a base, ignore the container and calculate the height from the size of base.

Using plastic foam

Plastic foam should be at least 5 cm (2 in) above the rim of the container for easier arranging. It will hold all light foliage stems, which should be cut on the slant for easier penetration of the foam. It does not take long to soak the foam. Place it in deep warm water and when it is completely saturated, it will sink just beneath the surface. A small round takes five to six minutes; a large block, about fifteen minutes. Foam anchors and pinholders should be firmly fixed to the containers. All components should be absolutely dry before applying a fixative, such as plasticine or proprietary adhesives such as 'Oasis-fix' which is a sticky 2.5 cm (1 in) wide strip, protected by waxed paper. A few centimetres bought from the florist will last for months.

'oasis-fix' in waxed paper

two ways of applying 'oasis-fix' to a foam anchor or pinholder

Using a pinholder

You will find that as you put material onto a pinholder it is either impaled on, or wedged between, the pins. This does not matter as long as the stems are held firmly in position. Hard thin stems should be cut on the slant and the pointed end pressed down hard onto the pinholder and pulled slightly backwards to give better hold. A larger stem needs to be split to allow the pin to penetrate it and the largest may need two splits at right angles to each other.

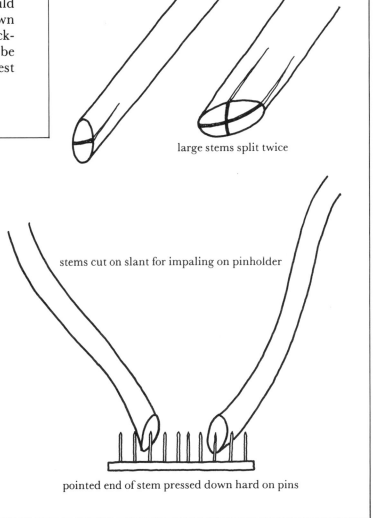

hard stems split once

large stems split twice

stems cut on slant for impaling on pinholder

pointed end of stem pressed down hard on pins

cut on slant with scissors

Aftercare

Water should be added to your arrangement daily or the flowers will soon wilt in a dry hot room. Using a long-spouted vessel, trickle water over the foam. It is safer to take the arrangement to the kitchen sink to do this to avoid splashing furniture or spilling water on the floor. The arrangement should be placed away from direct light, strong sunlight, draughts, and sources of heat such as the television set, a lamp, or a fire. The use of a fine spray of warm water helps to keep the flowers fresh.

If you want your arrangement to keep for a longer time, remove it to a cool place at night. The average life for flowers is four or five days; most foliage lasts longer.

Some popular arrangements

As mentioned earlier, arrangements fall into several distinct styles. These can be broadly described as mass or traditional; modern or free-form; naturalistic; and pot-et-fleur.

Mass or traditional

This is a design which uses a lot of plant material. Within the design there is little space, the flowers being quite close together, but without being overcrowded. It is sometimes termed 'bouquet anglais'. In Victorian times it was a rather cluttered design, but today it is arranged more loosely in geometric shapes, with plant material falling naturally, and with the flower heads having more room. This has been made possible by the use of plastic foam, which supports stems firmly in their arranged positions. Formerly, a deep urn-shaped vase filled with wire netting was employed. The urn shape is still used, but with a wedge of plastic foam protruding above rim level. Unseen containers (foam-filled saucers or empty tins on covered bases), baskets with lids or handles, wooden boxes (tea caddies or sewing boxes) may all be utilised for traditional designs. A traditional arrangement must appear to radiate from the centre where the largest and most beautiful flower is placed. In other words, from the point of interest.

A traditional design should have a recognisable shape. To obtain this we make a strong *outline* using narrow foliage. With the larger flowers we create an *area of interest* in the centre from which all stems appear to radiate. The centre and the outline are joined with graduated shapes, in other words leaves and flowers becoming larger towards the centre. These are the '*transitional* shapes'. Shorter pieces of this outline foliage are placed towards the centre of the arrangement between the larger flowers and leaves, to help in the transition from the small flowers near the outline to the largest at the centre of interest.

This procedure is known as 'bringing the outline material through the arrangement'. It ensures that the narrow material is not isolated on the boundary of the design, but continues to the centre, helping with the three-dimensional appearance and giving unity to the arrangement (see step 5 page 41). *Recessing* is also used to give a three-dimensional effect (see steps 4 and 5 page 41).

Modern or free-form

Modern or free-form is, as the name suggests, of the present time. This design breaks with tradition. It does not radiate from a central point. The emphasis is on strong line material, using natural sculptural shapes and contrasts. For instance, sword-like leaves of *Phormium tenax* or Iris leaves with large, rounded leaves of *Hosta* and *Bergenia*. A minimum of plant material is essential, and the impact of strong colour is often used, such as enchantment lilies, *Gerbera* and *Strelitzia*.

There may be more than one point of interest, but the design must balance both sides of an imaginary line through the centre of the arrangement. To judge, look with half-closed eyes. You may find that a bright flower on one side can be balanced by the addition of a larger leaf or several leaves on the opposite side. Because of the small amount of plant material, a pin-holder in a small container is the most suitable type of mechanics.

Naturalistic

Landscape designs can be considered as three-dimensional miniature pictures. They are easy and enjoyable to construct at any season of the year, and the choice of scenes unlimited – mountain, water-side, summer and winter themes are just a few of the possible subjects. They are inexpensive, and all the plant material can be freely obtained. However, a word of warning: use materials sparingly – a mossy bank needs only the suggestion of moss, do not clutter the whole base. Branches with too much growth will need to have some leaves pruned to give a better shape. When using accessories scale is important, too; if using a figurine, think of yourself in relation to the size of a tree. Shiny china accessories are unsuitable; use more naturalistic wood or pottery. The container in these arrangements is usually unseen unless water forms part of the landscape. The base should be of natural material such as wood or stone, and plant material should be in keeping with the type of landscape.

Pot-et-fleur

Pot-et-fleur arrangements combine growing plants with cut flowers. It is sensible to choose plants that enjoy the same growing conditions as each other and that are suitable for the chosen position in the room. For example, plants with variegated leaves need

plenty of light or the leaves will lose their attractive colouring, while ferns and ivies do not like bright sunshine. Select a variety of plants: one with a plain green foliage and one with variegated or coloured leaves, a fine tall plant and one that trails over the rim of the container. As in a flower arrangement, the width of the design must be balanced by its height. If the plants are not tall enough this may be remedied by adding tall flowers or a piece of driftwood placed upright. The surface may be covered with stones, moss or shells to hide the compost and to add extra interest.

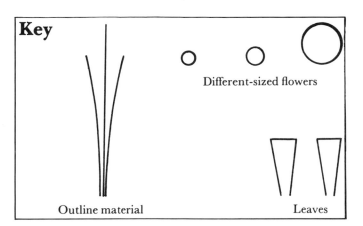

Key

Outline material

Different-sized flowers

Leaves

Traditional arrangements

Symmetrical triangle

No. 1 stem – One-and-a-half times the height or width of container, plus 5 cm (2 in) to allow for insertion of stem into foam.

Nos. 2 and 3 stems – Two-thirds the length of No. 1 stem; place in the front of the foam, about 2.5 cm (1 in) from each side, pointing downwards over the rim of the container.

Nos. 4 and 5 stems – Half the length of No. 2 stem, place at the back of the arrangement, in the same position as Nos. 2 and 3 stems.

Nos. 6 and 7 stems – 4 to 5 cm (1½–2 in) shorter than No. 1 stem.

Nos. 8 and 9 stems – 3 cm (1 in or so) shorter than Nos. 6 and 7.

This forms the outline. All additional flowers and foliage must be shorter in order to keep the triangular shape.

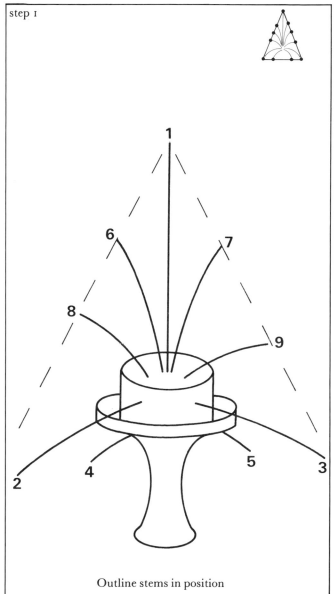

step 1

Outline stems in position

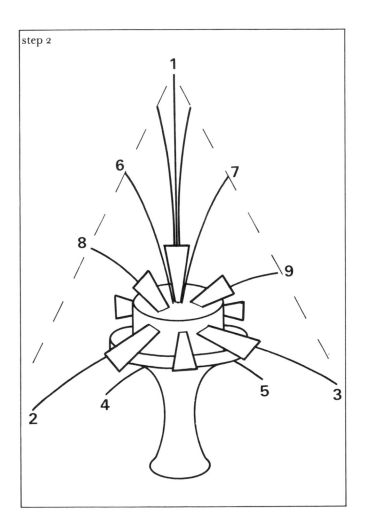

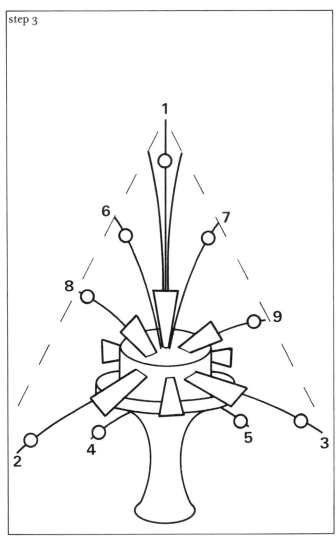

Strengthen No. 1 stem by the addition of one or two pieces of outline material. To make a background for the flowers and to hide the foam, add larger leaves as shown in the diagram. Insert two or three leaves at the back, and at the base of No. 1 stem to keep the arrangement balanced.

Small flowers are now added. If possible they should be almost as long as the outline material.

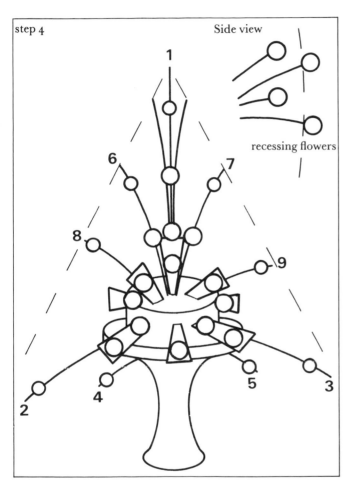

step 4

Side view

recessing flowers

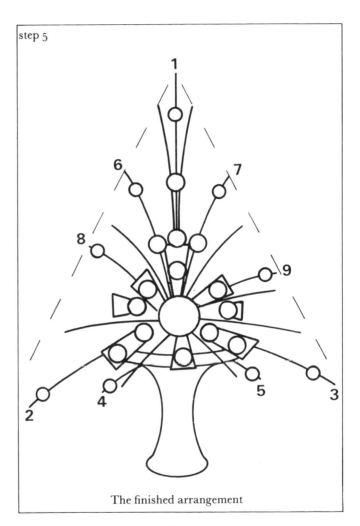

step 5

The finished arrangement

More flowers are added, progressively larger towards the centre and with the pattern keeping within the guidelines of the outline material. Do not arrange all the flowers facing forward; turn some sideways to give a more natural appearance. Neither must they all be placed at the same level; some should be cut shorter and pushed lower into the foam. This is called recessing.

Recess the largest flower in the centre of the arrangement. If you do not have a large flower, a cluster of blooms may be used. Add some outline foliage between the flowers. With recessing, this helps to give a three-dimensional appearance and adds bulk to the finished arrangement.

Asymmetrical triangle

In this arrangement the sides are unequal. The longest side can be either on the left or the right of the design. This shape is used when there is an unequal amount of wall space; for example, in a corner where there is more room along one wall. When used on the right-hand side of a mantelshelf the shorter side is to the right, with the longer placement flowing in toward the centre. If used on the left, then the shorter side is to the left of the arrangement.

No. 1 stem – One-and-a-half times the height or width of the container plus 5 cm (2 in) to allow for insertion of stem into the foam.

No. 2 stem – One-third or one-half the length of No. 3 stem.

No. 3 stem – Two-thirds the length of No. 1 stem.

No. 4 stem – One-half the length of No. 2 stem.

No. 5 stem – One-half the length of No. 3 stem.

Nos. 6 and 7 stems – About 5 cm (1 ½ to 2 in) shorter than No. 1 stem.

Nos. 8 and 9 stems – About 3 cm (1 in) or so shorter than Nos. 6 and 7 stems.

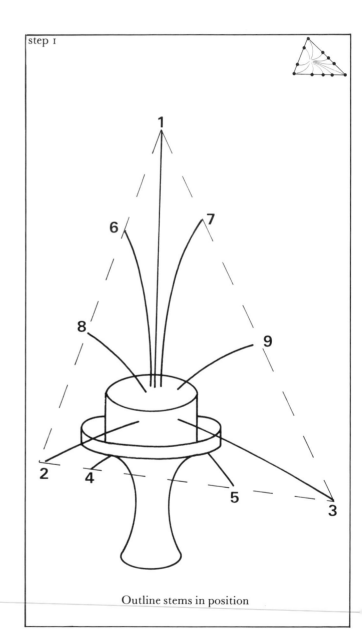

step 1

Outline stems in position

42

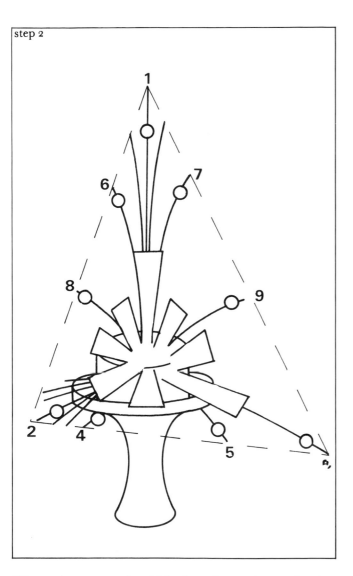

No. 2 placement should be heavier and more bushy, to balance the long No. 3 stem. Small flowers are placed in position.

Steps 3 and 4 are the same as for the symmetrical triangle. The centre of interest is still at the base of No. 1 stem, where the largest and most important flower, or a cluster of flowers, is recessed.

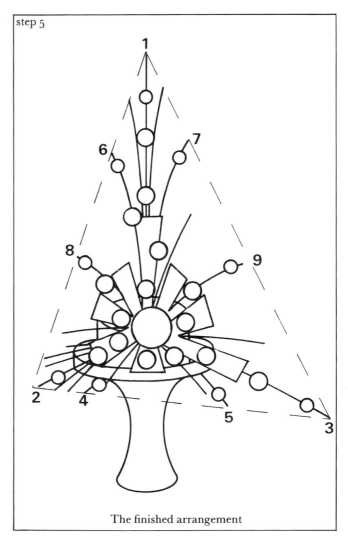

The finished arrangement

Vertical arrangement

This is a slim elegant arrangement having a strong upward movement. Specific plant material is mentioned here because only certain types of plant give the correct finished appearance.

Outline material Irises, yucca, pampas, gladioli, bulrushes and any other plants with tall slender growth are suitable for use in a vertical arrangement.

Transitional material Attractive large leaves for the base of the arrangement include *Bergenia*, *Hosta*, foxglove and honesty.

Flowers Irises, lilies, gladioli, larkspur, roses and chrysanthemums provide the most useful flowers for this type of design.

One central placement of slender leaves (such as iris) may be inserted into plastic foam or onto a pinholder and wire netting. The height of the central leaf should be more than twice the height or width of the container, whichever is the greater.

step 2

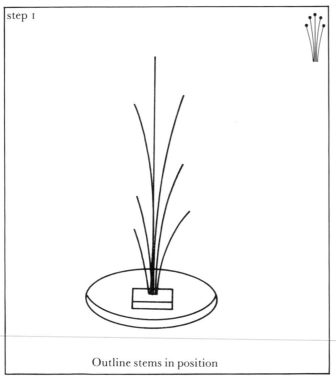

step I

Outline stems in position

Insert large leaves at the base of the central placement, both in front and at the back to give the arrangement a stable-looking base to balance the height.

Add flowers. The tallest and smallest flowers should be almost as long as the central placement. Continue adding flowers, keeping the design slim and uncluttered until the base is reached. Recess larger ones in the centre and place smaller ones to the outer edges of the container to produce the finished arrangement.

L-shaped arrangement

An L-shaped arrangement may be placed at either or both ends of a mantelshelf, in a corner position or a window sill. It is a useful shape for church windows, embellishing without hiding the design on the stained glass. It is also a good design to complement a rectangular picture or photograph. Specific plant material is mentioned here because only certain types of plant give the correct finished appearance.

Outline material   Tall or upward growth, such as iris, yucca, delphinium, *Artemisia* and *Atroplex* is suitable.

Flowers   Roses, carnations and chrysanthemums.

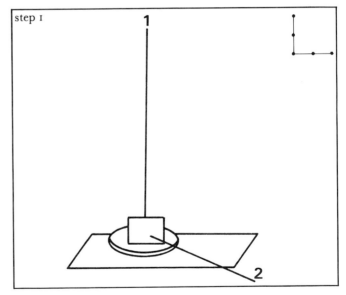

This design may be arranged in a small container with foam or pinholder, and wire netting placed on a larger base. The base is now considered to be the container, and the height of the design should be about twice the width of the base.

No. 2 stem is about two-thirds the length of No. 1 stem. *Note* the angle of the No. 2 stem; it is positioned at an angle of 45 degrees to the front. This gives a more pleasing arrangement than if it were positioned to point straight ahead.

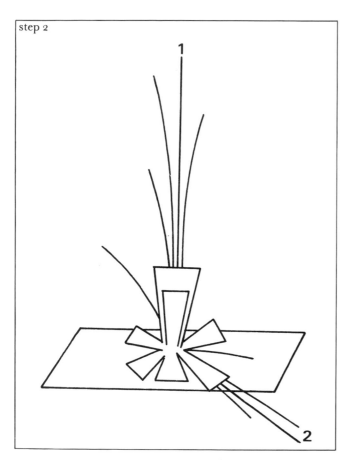

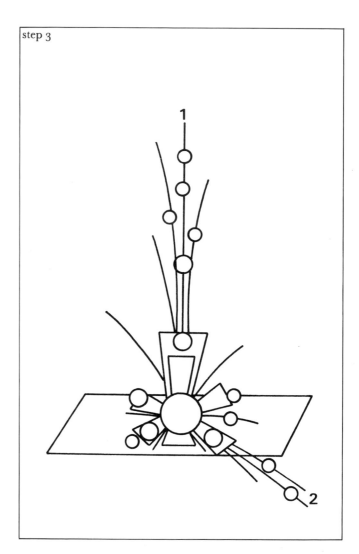

Strengthen No. 1 and No. 2 stems by adding more outline material. Insert some larger leaves at the base for balance.

Finish the design by adding the flowers as in the diagram, with the small flowers nearer the extremities of the design. Insert some outline material between the leaves and flowers to complete the design.

Horizontal arrangement

This is a long low design suitable for a dining table, with or without candles, or for a radiator shelf or window sill.

Outline material Any straight-growing, small-leaved foliage or flower spray such as privet or *Antirrhinum*, gives suitable outline material.

Transitional material *Mahonia* has good-sized leaves for the centre of the arrangement.

Flowers Spray chrysanthemums, daisy-like blooms, roses and carnations.

The best type of container for a horizontal arrangement is an oval or oblong one, and it may be seen or hidden. The arrangement can be of any length that suits the allocated space. The size of the arrangement for a dining table depends upon the size of the table itself, the place-mats, and the number of guests. It can be up to one-fifth of the table length. The width should not be more than one-third of the whole arrangement. Such a long low design should not be more than 20 cm (8 in) tall including the height of the container. The foam should be at least 3 cm (1 in or so) above the rim of the container for easy arranging.

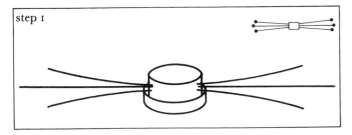

Arrange the outline material: if fine, several pieces of foliage may be necessary in each outline placement. Insert two pieces of outline material at centre front and back.

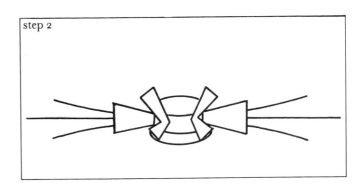

Add two large leaves, one at either end, along the outline length and four smaller leaves towards the centre, over the edge of the foam, two to the front and two to the back, as in the diagram. These help to hide the mechanics and provide a background for the flowers added in step 3.

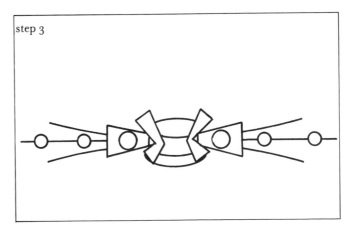

Begin inserting the flowers, the longest and smallest at each end, increasing in size towards the centre.

47

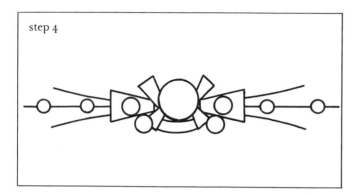

step 4

The centre flowers are added, one large bloom in the very centre and one slightly smaller to the right and left, forward over the container. As this arrangement is for the middle of the table, turn it around and insert the same number of flowers in the other side.

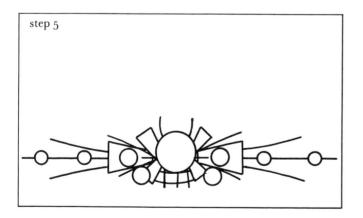

step 5

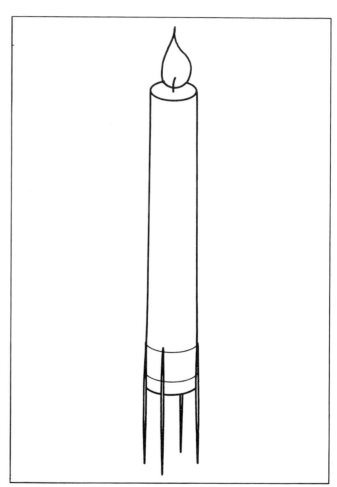

Add some outline material at the centre between the flowers to unify the design.

For table arrangements you may like to have a candle at the centre of the design. The best way to insert the candle into the foam, in order to avoid making a large hole in it, is to stick four cocktail sticks around the base of the candle with adhesive tape and insert the sticks into the foam until the end of the candle rests on the foam.

Circular all-round arrangement

A circular arrangement is suitable for a low oval or round table or for a table decoration at dinner. To ensure a symmetrical arrangement, think of the container as a clock face and place *five* pieces of outline material horizontally at 12-minute intervals as in the diagram of step 1.

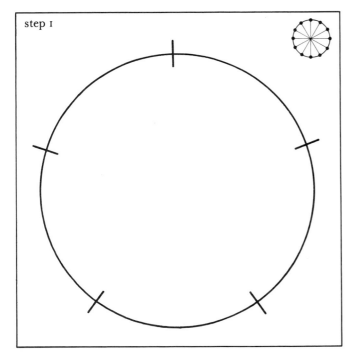

The five outline stems should be about one half to two-thirds the width of the container. The sixth stem, which should be slightly shorter than the other five if it is viewed from above, is placed vertically in the centre of the foam. If a candle replaces this central stem, it must be 25 to 30 cm (10 to 12 in) high so as to be well above the level of the plant material.

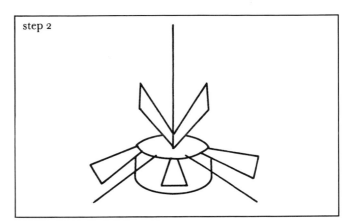

Between each of the five stems of outline material, place a large leaf, and also place some leaves in the centre to cover the foam and give body to the arrangement.

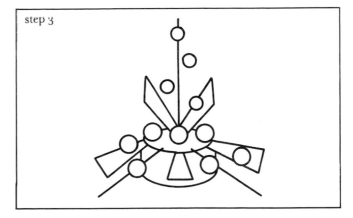

The largest flowers are placed along the lower edge, gradually becoming smaller as they reach the top of the design to form a conical shape.

Curving designs

The most suitable material for crescent-shaped arrangements is provided by those plants that grow naturally in a curving manner, for example *Escallonia* and broom. Broom is very useful as it can be manipulated easily, without looking contrived. Most foliage branches can be encouraged to curve a little more if warmed in the hands and bent gently at the same time.

The container may be a small saucer shape or a larger flat bowl, depending on the size of table or piece of furniture on which it is to be placed. Pinholders and wire netting are the most suitable mechanics to use as the width of the finished arrangement should only be one-third of the total length. Plastic foam can be used, but as it is hard to hide in this design only a small piece should be employed.

Crescent shapes have many uses. An *inverted crescent* is a formal design that looks elegant on a dinner table. A *shallow crescent* looks well on a table below eye level. A plate-picture or mirror can be complemented by a crescent that follows the same lines.

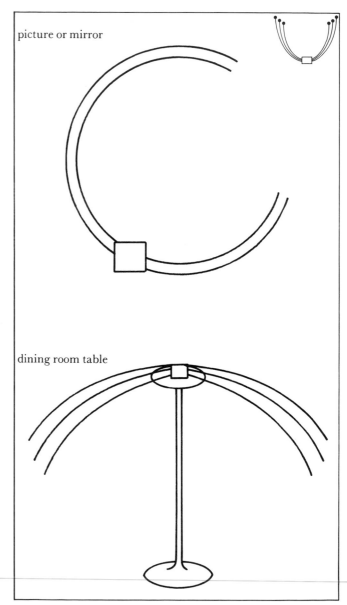

picture or mirror

dining room table

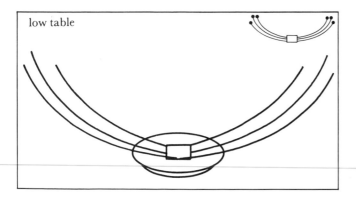

low table

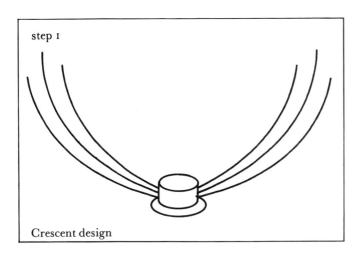

step 1

Crescent design

First the outline material is encouraged to curve and then positioned to form a shallow curve as in diagram.

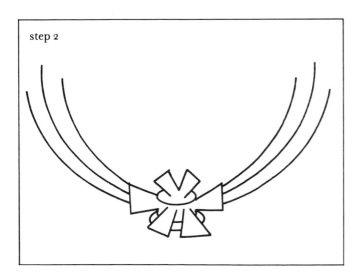

step 2

Large leaves are added at the centre of interest.

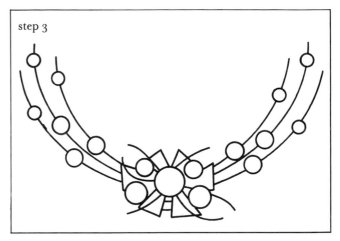

step 3

Small flowers are placed at the ends of the crescent with the larger flowers placed in the centre.

Finally short pieces of outline material are brought through the whole arrangement to the centre of interest.

The method of arrangment is the same for all the variations of crescent design. First the outline material is encouraged to curve, and is then positioned to form an arc. Large leaves are added at the centre of interest. Small flowers are placed at the ends of the crescent with the larger flowers placed in the centre. Finally, outline material is brought through the whole arrangement to the centre of interest.

Hogarth curve

Sometimes referred to as a lazy S, the elegant Hogarth curve may be arranged to curve either from left to right or right to left, whichever is most suitable for the location you have in mind. Naturally curving plant material is essential in the design, and the container should be tall to accommodate the downward curve – a candlestick with a candlecup is very suitable. The plastic foam should be about 3 cm (1 in or so) above the rim of the container and quite small in diameter, as the width at the centre of the design should be only one-third of the total length of the arrangement.

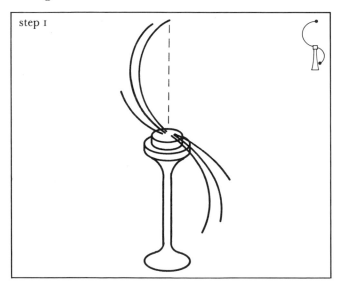

No. 1 stem – May be up to one-and-a-half times the
  height of the container.

No. 2 stem – Two-thirds the length of No. 1 stem.

Add one or two more curving stems to make a strongly defined outline.

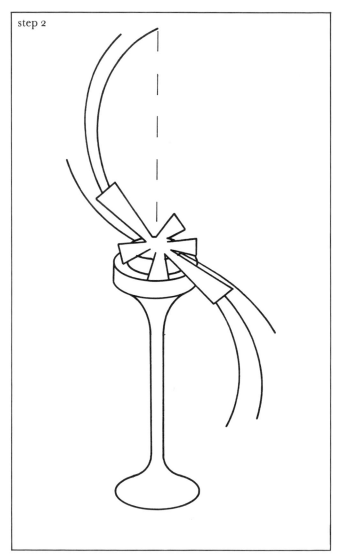

Large leaves are added to the outline, and in the centre, to hide the foam and to provide a background for the flowers at the point of interest.

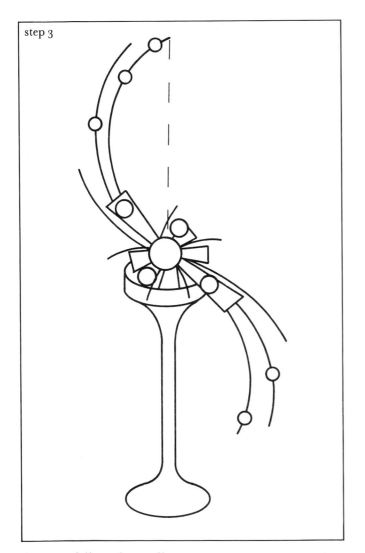

step 3

It is most important to have the tip of No. 1 stem directly over the point of interest to give balance to the design.

Flowers follow the outline material, the largest being recessed in the centre and the smallest at the tips of the curve. Finish by including some outline material at the centre.

Basket arrangements

The basket used should not be deep, otherwise it is difficult to obtain a good shape to the design. The handle should be fairly high so that it is visible in the arrangement. This also applies to the lid, if it has one. An informal loose arrangement is best; it may be triangular or horizontal in shape, but the plant material should be allowed to flow naturally over the edge of the basket for the best effect.

A container with plastic foam is suitable except for spring bulbs, which need shallow water and for which a pinholder and wire netting are called for. Keep the container in position by attaching it to the handles, or through the basket weave, with string or a piece of wire.

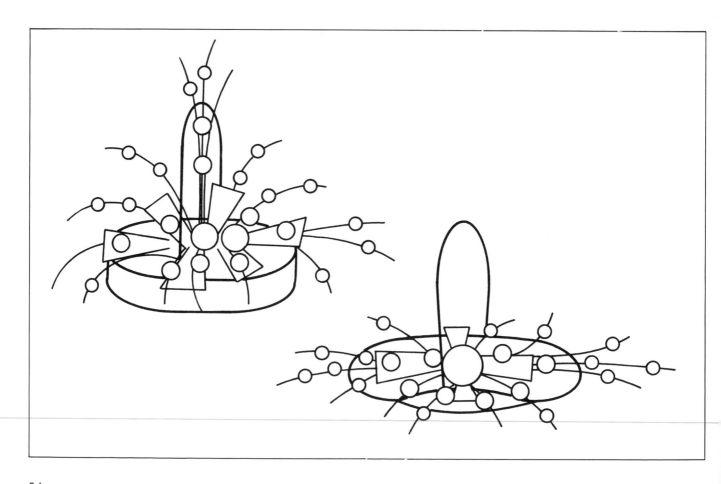

Landscape designs

Landscape designs are the most naturalistic type of flower arrangement. A shallow dish of pottery or glass is a suitable container for water scenes.

The plants should be those which grow in or beside the water such as alder, willow, rushes, iris, water-lily etc.

Pot-et-fleur arrangement

This is an arrangement of growing plants combined with cut flowers. It is very suitable for centrally heated rooms. The plants last a long time and the fresh flowers can be added and replaced when necessary. It is also a useful winter arrangement when fresh flowers are hard to come by and very expensive to buy.

The container should be sufficiently deep to allow the plant roots to be well below the rim for ease in watering. It should also be large enough to hold several plants. A small container for the cut flowers is placed between the plants. It can contain a pinholder, wire netting or plastic foam to support the flowers. A cigar or pill tube is also useful to hold flowers. Mounted on a short piece of cane it can be anchored between the growing plants, and can easily be filled with water for the flowers.

Preparation

It is essential to provide drainage for the plants. A layer of washed gravel or broken crocks is placed in the bottom of the container and covered with a 2.5 cm (1 in) layer of John Innes No. 2 Compost. To remove the plants from their pots, carefully loosen any roots that might be protruding through the drainage holes in the bottom, squeeze the plastic pot all the way round and turn it upside down. If the plant does not fall into your hand, knock the pot on the side of a table. The plants, together with the cut flower container, are placed in the layer of compost. Arrange the plants so that the tallest is at the back. Add more compost and press the plants firmly in position. Continue covering until the soil is about 3 cm (1 in or so) from the rim.

Aftercare

The plants will require the same care as individual house plants. Be careful not to over-water them. Occasionally wipe the dust from the leaves or spray with lukewarm water. Do remember to top up the water in the cut-flower containers.

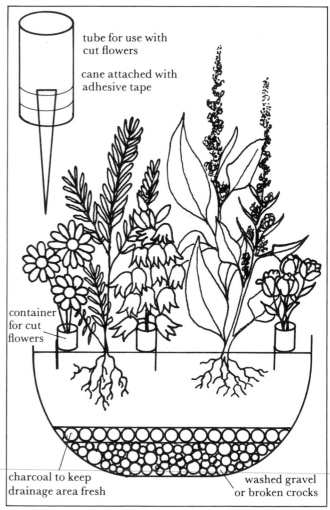

tube for use with cut flowers

cane attached with adhesive tape

container for cut flowers

charcoal to keep drainage area fresh

washed gravel or broken crocks

Step-by-step arrangements

The arrangements in the photographic section which follows are all based on the step-by-step explanatory drawings described earlier. Even though you may be inexperienced in flower arranging, I would encourage you to allow your own personality and style to develop. Given the same instructions to follow, and similar plant material, no two people will produce identical arrangements.

To give you an idea of size, all plant material used in the finished arrangements has been measured. Metric, and approximate imperial units, are both given. Do not cut *all* your foliage and flowers to these measurements before starting your design. Measure and cut only the outline pieces and then cut the rest as necessary, following the step-by-step guide. Place flowers and foliage in the position where they flow most naturally; for instance, plant material curving to the right should be inserted so as to fall to the right-hand side of the arrangement. Above all, do not try to imitate every detail of these arrangements; an imaginative touch adds interest. Finally, the type of arrangement is indicated by the outline key shape.

This design is treated as two vertical arrangements (see page 44). 'A' has 6 narcissi flowers and 8 leaves of different lengths, and 'B' has 4 sprays of forsythia and 6 narcissi leaves. The narcissi leaves are common to both placements, and are the link which unites the design.

Two-placement arrangement

Height 63 cm (25 in)

Components
Oval ovenware glass dish 30.5 cm (12 in) long × 23 cm (9 in) wide × 5 cm (2 in) deep
2 × 6.5 cm (2½ in) diameter pinholders
1 long narrow stone 12.5 cm (5 in) long × 5 cm (2 in) wide

Foliage
14 narcissi leaves
Placement 'A' 8 leaves
2 × 25.5 cm (10 in),
4 × 20 cm (8 in),
1 × 15 cm (6 in), 1 × 12.5 cm (5 in)

Placement 'B' 6 leaves
2 × 24 cm (9½ in), 1 × 21 cm (8½ in), 3 × 18 cm (7 in)

Flowers
Placement 'A' 6 narcissi
1 × 34 cm (13½ in), 1 × 32 cm (12½ in), 2 × 30.5 cm (12 in), 1 × 23 cm (9 in), 1 × 20 cm (8 in)
Placement 'B' 4 sprays flowering forsythia
1 × 46 cm (18 in), 1 × 53 cm (21 in), 1 × 63 cm (25 in) 1 × 76 cm (30 in)

Step 1

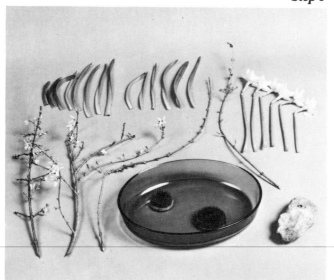

Step 2

The 76 cm (30 in) forsythia stem has been placed at the back of 'B', brought around 'A', and inserted in front of 'B' The arrangement would be complete without this stem but, as it was available, it was added for extra interest.

The large stone, besides hiding the mechanics, emphasises the unity or 'oneness' of the design. Pinholders completely submerged in water go unnoticed.

Place on an occasional table or somewhere with a clear background for maximum effect.

Step 3

Step 4

Step 5

Finish

This arrangement needs very little explanation. It was designed specially to complement the picture in the background. The outline was made using two of the iris stems; No. 1 stem is 51 cm (20 in); No. 2 stem 28 cm (11 in). The third iris, 16.5 cm (6½ in), was placed with the large leaves at the base to give colour balance (see step 2, below). As can be seen from the photo-

'L'-shape

Height 58.5 cm (23 in)

Components
Green velvet base 35 cm (14 in) × 20 cm (8 in)
Foam dish with foam round

Foliage
iris foliage
8 *Aucuba* leaves (measured from tip of leaf to end of stem)
1 × 35 cm (14 in), 2 × 20 cm (8 in), 2 × 18 cm (7 in), 2 × 15 cm (6 in), 1 × 12.5 cm (5 in)
7 ferns
1 × 33 cm (13 in), 3 × 24 cm (9½ in), 2 × 12.5 cm (5 in), 1 × 20 cm (8 in)

Flowers
6 irises
1 × 51 cm (20 in), 2 × 28 cm (11 in), 1 × 18 cm (7 in), 1 × 16.5 cm (6½ in)
9 narcissi
1 × 49.5 cm (19½ in), 1 × 44.5 cm (17½ in), 2 × 28 cm (11 in), 1 × 21 cm (8½ in), 1 × 20 cm (8 in), 1 × 15 cm (6 in), 2 × 14 cm (5½ in)

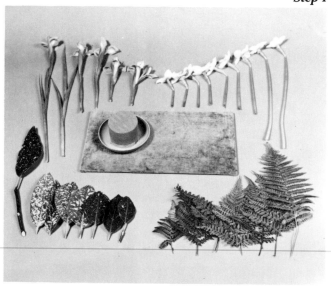

Step 1

Step 2

graphs below, 2 irises with 3 narcissi complete the centre, while the remaining narcissi follow the outline.

The completed arrangement was raised on a piece of wood 15 cm (6 in) × 10 cm (4 in) × 1 cm (½ in) deep. Even a small space between the base and the table gives interesting shadow and a lighter effect.

Step 3

Step 4

Step 5

Finish

Small spring flowers look attractive arranged in a box. The mechanics of the design were a 6.5 cm (2½ in) pinholder, stuck to the metal lining with an adhesive. Wire netting, 4 cm (1½ in) gauge, was pushed on to the pinholder using the closed blades of the flower scissors. The lid was propped open by a cut stem impaled on the pinholder.

The outline was made with periwinkle sprays, strengthened

Welcome to spring

Height 30.5 cm (12 in)

Components
Box with lid, black japanned 23 cm (9 in) long × 15 cm (6 in) wide × 5 cm (2 in) deep
Box lining – a metal tin – 15 cm (6 in) × 10 cm (4 in) × 6 cm (2½ in)
6.5 cm (2½ in) diameter pinholder
Small piece of crumpled chicken wire

Foliage
4 sprays of periwinkle
1 × 28 cm (11 in), 1 × 23 cm (9 in), 1 × 18 cm (7 in), 1 × 16.5 cm (6½ in)
8 daffodil leaves; 3 bundles of various heights
Bundle 1: 1 × 25.5 cm (10 in), 1 × 18 cm (7 in), 1 × 16.5 cm (6½ in)
Bundle 2: 1 × 20 cm (8 in), 1 × 19 cm (7½ in), 1 × 18 cm (7 in)
Bundle 3: 1 × 15 cm (6 in), 1 × 12.5 cm (5 in)

Flowers
14 crocuses
Bunch of 4 (white), each 12.5 cm (5 in)
Bunch of 4 (purple), each 12.5 cm (5 in)
Bunch of 6 (yellow), each 14 cm (5½ in)
8 lily of the valley
8 × 16.5 cm (6½ in)
5 small flowered daffodils – 1 × 25.5 cm (10 in), 1 × 20 cm (8 in), 1 × 18 cm (7 in), 1 × 15 cm (6 in), 1 × 12.5 cm (5 in)

Step 1

Step 2

by the addition of daffodil leaves. Apart from the daffodil flowers, all the other small flowers have been made into bundles with rubber bands and inserted as blocks of colour to give impact. Spring flowers, being soft stemmed, are more easily arranged in water and held in place with wire netting.

A suitable desk arrangement for the man of the house.

Step 3

Step 4

Step 5

Finish

Flowers in the bedroom give an extra welcome to a guest. On this occasion they were arranged to complement the oval mirror on the dressing table.

The plastic foam is narrower than the container but is 2.5 cm (1 in) above the rim. Only a small piece is necessary, as the finished arrangement must not be too wide at the centre (see the step-by-step illustrations below. Remember also that the back will be visible in the mirror.

Greetings

Height 40.5 cm (16 in)

Components
Sardine-type tin 10 cm (4 in) long × 6.5 cm (2½ in) wide × 4 cm (1½ in) deep, covered with pink material to match flowers
Plastic foam 7.5 cm (3 in) long × 5 cm (2 in) wide × 6.5 cm (2½ in) deep

Foliage
13 *Prunus pissardii* sprays (in bloom)
1 × 35.5 cm (14 in), 1 × 28 cm (11 in), 2 × 20 cm (8 in), 3 × 18 cm (7 in), 4 × 15 cm (6 in), 2 × 12.5 (5 in)
8 tellima leaves
2 × 18 cm (7 in), 1 × 15 cm (6 in), 2 × 11.5 cm (4½ in), 3 × 7.5 cm (3 in)

Flowers
5 tulips
1 × 23 cm (9 in), 2 × 15 cm (6 in), 2 × 11.5 cm (4½ in)

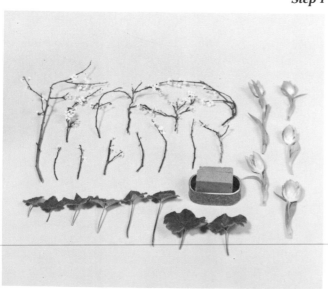

Step 1

Step 2

The outline is of *Prunus pissardii*, and the transitional material of tellima leaves. Three smaller tulips follow the outline shape, the point of interest being made up of the remaining 2 tulips and tellima leaves, with some short pieces of outline material. This is a great deal of plant material for a small piece of foam.

Do remember to top up daily with water (see aftercare, page 36).

Step 3

Step 4

Step 5

Finish

Before starting, remember to fill the bottle with water. This slender arrangement is about twice the height of the container.

Hold the first iris flower in the bottle and decide how tall you want it. The stem need not reach the bottom as it can be wedged at the required height. Add the second iris bloom, together with foliage, and adjust for height. Still holding the stems, place the two tellima leaves at the neck edge, one slanting backwards and the other slanting forwards. Insert a wedge; in this case a piece of iris stem was used.

The bottle was placed on a shiny bronze wall tile, 15 cm (6 in) × 15 cm (6 in), to link up with the bronze colouring on the leaves. Reflections in the water added sparkle to the design. Any well-defined leaves may be used, for instance *Bergenia* or *Hosta*.

Roses arranged in this way, with their own foliage, look particularly lovely. Chrysanthemums can be substituted for a winter design.

An arrangement suitable for the dining area or a living room.

Keep it narrow

Height 53.5 cm (21 in)

Components
Green wine bottle 25.5 cm (10 in) high
Wall tile 15 cm (6 in) × 15 cm (6 in)

Foliage
2 tellima leaves, each 11.5 cm (4½ in)
Iris foliage from two flowers
Iris stem 12.5 cm (5 in) long (used as wedge)

Flowers
2 irises
1 × 53.5 cm (21 in), 1 × 35 cm (14 in)

Step 1

Finish

The well pinholder, filled with water, was placed off centre, towards the back of the wood slice base. The golden alder branch was impaled on the pinholder (see the illustration below), and the primrose leaves inserted at the base. Driftwood was placed in front, covering the edge of the pinholder, and the flowers were arranged in a natural manner behind the driftwood. Moss was added at the front and some to the side to hide the mechanics.

A plain background is necessary to show a landscape to advantage.

Hint of spring

Height 66 cm (26 in)

Components
Irregular-shaped wood slice 37 cm (14½ in) long × 15 cm (6 in) wide × 2.5 cm (1 in) depth
Well pinholder
Small piece of driftwood

Foliage
Golden alder branch 61 cm (24 in) long
4 primrose leaves, various sizes, 11.5 cm (4½ in) long

Flowers
3 primroses 7.5 cm (3 in) long

Step 1

Finish

67

This arrangement was constructed in wet foam impaled on a pinholder and extending 4–5 cm (1½–2 in) above the rim of the container. The cream pedestal-type ceramic urn was 12.5 cm (5 in) high and 18 cm (7 in) wide, so the height of the arrangement was calculated from the width measurement. When using fine outline material it is sometimes necessary to increase the length of the No. 1 stem to give a more balanced and elegant design. In this case it was increased by about 7.5 cm (3 in). With practice you will soon master this point. If you are disatisfied when you have finished a vertical or triangular arrangement, try adding a

From garden and countryside   Height 48 cm (19 in)

Components
Pedestal-type ceramic vase
12.5 cm (5 in) high × 18 cm
(7 in) wide
Plastic foam mounted on a
foam anchor

Foliage
12 pieces of pussy willow
1 × 38 cm (15 in), 1 × 35.5
cm (14 in), 2 × 28 cm (11
in), 5 × 23 cm (9 in), 3 × 18
cm (7 in)
14 pieces of fern
1 × 30 cm (12 in), 2 × 25.5
cm (10 in), 2 × 23 cm (9 in),
2 × 20 cm (8 in), 3 × 18 cm

(7 in), 4 × 15 cm (6 in)
5 tulip leaves

Flowers
12 narcissi
2 × 25.5 cm (10 in), 1 × 28
cm (11 in), 1 × 20 cm (8 in),
3 × 16.5 cm (6½ in), 5 ×
12.5 cm (5 in)
5 two-tone tulips
1 × 20 cm (8 in), 2 × 18 cm
(7 in), 2 × 15 cm (6 in)
5 large red tulips
1 × 28 cm (11 in), 1 × 23
cm (9 in), 1 × 15 cm (6 in),
2 × 12.5 cm (5 in)

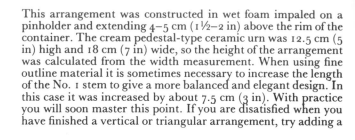

Step 1

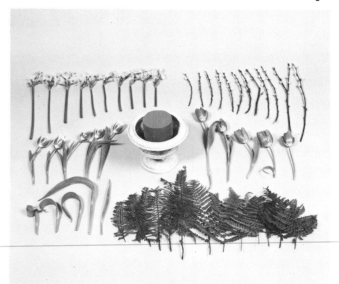

Step 2

longer stem for the No. 1 placement and decide whether you prefer the taller design.

The pussy willow was strengthened by the ferns, which followed the outline as well as acting as transitional material towards the centre (see page 37). Some were placed at the back to give stability. Three red tulips follow the No. 1 placement, 1 at 28 cm (11 in), 1 at 23 cm (9 in) and 1 at 15 cm (6 in), down the centre. The remaining two red tulips, 12.5 cm (5 in) each, followed lines 2 and 3 (see photograph below). The narcissi were placed between as transitional material. The five two-tone

tulips were then added to give extra colour where needed. The tulip leaves, rolled loosely (around a pencil) were inserted at the centre of interest for extra contrast and to hide the mechanics.

The finished arrangement made a focal point in the dining area placed on a shelf in the room divider.

Step 3

Step 4

Step 5

Finish

Ploughman's lunch

Height 53.5 cm (21 in)

The modern housewife very often entertains friends in the kitchen. This design was constructed at short notice for such an occasion.

A saucepan lid, turned upside down, was used as the container. It was chosen to contrast with the red tiled wall. The mechanics were a pinholder inside a food tin which had a strip of white card attached around it with adhesive tape, to match the colour of the lid. As can be seen in the photograph (below), the No. 1 placement in the centre was made up of three iris leaves 46 cm (18 in), 40 cm (16 in) and 35 cm (14 in), placed upright. The tops of all three were cut on the slant to give a more modern

Components

Upturned saucepan lid 19 cm (7½ in) diameter × 7 cm (2¾ in) high
Food tin 7.5 cm (3 in) diameter × 3 cm (1¼ in) deep – covered by a strip of white card to match saucepan lid
6.5 cm (2½ in) pinholder

Foliage

5 iris leaves
1 × 46 cm (18 in), 1 × 40 cm (16 in), 1 × 35.5 cm (14 in), 1 × 29 cm (11½ in), 1 × 24 cm (9½ in)
3 *Hosta* leaves

1 × stem length 10 cm (4 in) + leaf length 25.5 cm (10 in)
2 × stem length 5 cm (2 in) + leaf length 16.5 cm (6½ in)
1 spray nasturtium foliage 12.5 cm (5 in)

Flowers

7 nasturtiums, mixed colours of yellow and red
1 stem with 2 yellow flowers 25.5 cm (10 in)
1 red flower 15 cm (6 in)
1 yellow flower 7.5 cm (3 in)
2 red & 1 yellow flower 10 cm (4 in)

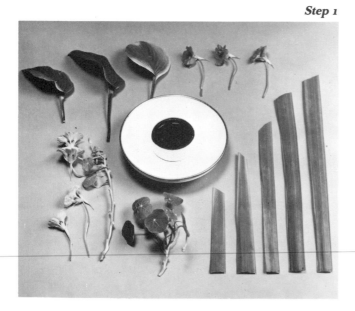

Step 1

Step 2

appearance. Two more leaves 29 cm (11½ in) and 24 cm (9½ in) were inserted at an angle, to the left and in front of the first placement. Two *Hosta* leaves were added, one on the right and one on the left, so as to give balance. The third was placed so as to fall forward over the rim of the container. Four nasturtium flowers made up the centre. Two 10 cm (4 in) flowers, with the 12.5 cm (5 in) nasturtium foliage spray, cascade over the edge of the container.

Do remember to fill pinholder tin with water before starting and as the container is so small it will need extra aftercare attention.

Step 3

Step 4

Step 5

Finish

Eleven sprays of sweet peas in mixed pastel colours with fifteen pieces of everlasting sweet pea foliage were arranged in a glass sugar bowl, criss-crossed over the top with adhesive tape (see below), and filled with water. Two pieces of foliage 23 cm (9 in) long, were inserted in the centre of the bowl. Ten stems were arranged as a border around, and extending over, the rim. The remaining three pieces at 23 cm (9 in) were placed at equal intervals between the centre and the edge. I used the everlasting sweet pea foliage because its luxuriant growth made hiding the

mechanics much easier. You may initially experience a slight difficulty in getting the centre pieces of foliage to stand upright but, as you continue to add more stems, you will find that you can adjust them quite easily. The flowers filled up the remaining spaces, making a Victorian-style posy.

The delicate structure of the sweet peas and the sparkle of the cut-glass bowl, make a happy combination. The Victorian atmosphere was further suggested by placing the arrangement on a small round table, complete with lace doily.

A posy for Great Grandma

Height 34 cm (13½ in)

Foliage
15 pieces of everlasting sweet pea foliage
5 × 23 cm (9 in), 10 × 7.5 cm (3 in)

Components
Glass sugar bowl 11.5 cm (4½ in) high × 14 cm (5½ in) diameter (i.e. pedestal type)
Sticky tape to criss-cross over top of the bowl

Flowers
11 sprays sweet peas, mixed pastel colours
2 × 23 cm (9 in), 3 × 18 cm (7 in), 6 × 12.5 cm (5 in)

Step 1

Finish

This is a quick and easy way to arrange an informal bunch of flowers:

The pottery jug was part-filled with broken foam and topped with crushed wire netting, cut ends uppermost, and then filled with water. The longest piece of foliage was inserted in the centre and held in position by wrapping a cut end of the wire netting around the stem. The other pieces were arranged around the rim to make a background for the flowers. The summer stocks and

the irises were pushed in at different heights, and the roses added between them, with some towards the centre for interest. The pastel flowers contrasted well with the dark blue jug.

An arrangement suitable for a table in the hall or a large sitting room.

A mixed bunch

Height 61 cm (24 in)

Components
Dark blue jug (containing broken foam and crushed wire netting)
18 cm (7 in) high × 11.5 cm (4½ in) diameter at top

Foliage
6 pieces of *Euonymus japonica*
1 × 48 cm (19 in), 2 × 40.5 cm (16 in), 1 × 30.5 cm (12 in), 1 × 28 cm (11 in), 1 × 25.5 cm (10 in)

Flowers
3 delphiniums each 48 cm (19 in)
5 roses
1 × 35.5 (14 in), 1 × 30.5 cm (12 in), 2 × 28 cm (11 in), 1 × 25.5 cm (10 in)
3 irises
1 × 40.5 cm (16 in), 2 × 28 cm (11 in)
6 summer stocks
(11 in), 1 × 25.5 cm (10 in) 25.5 cm (10 in)

Step 1

Finish

Fever few, with acid-green foliage, arranged with single, white, daisy-like flowered spray chrysanthemums, can glow in a dark corner and highlight a room.

Simple flowers look best in a simple container, so a water-filled cereal bowl was chosen, together with a pinholder 6 cm (2½ in) in diameter, and crumpled wire netting held in place with a rubber band. The leaves of fever few were arranged around the edge of the bowl. The centre placement was a 25.5 cm (10 in) stem of chrysanthemum with four blooms. Five larger-

For a dark corner

Height 29 cm (11½ in)

Components
Cereal bowl 5.5 cm (2¼ in)
high × 15 cm (6 in)
diameter
2 oz food tin 3 cm (1¼ in)
high × 7.5 cm (3 in)
diameter – to raise the
finished arrangement
Pinholder
Wire netting held in place
with rubber band

Foliage
4 sprays of feverfew, each
15 cm (6 in)

10 single leaves of feverfew,
each 15 cm (6 in)

Flowers
6 sprays *Alchemilla*, each 18
cm (7 in)
2 stems of spray
chrysanthemums, to give 18
various sized blooms

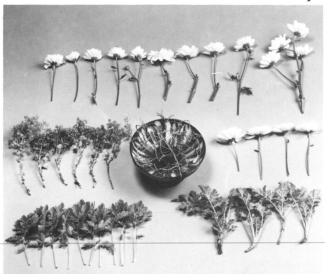

Step 1

Step 2

sized blooms 17.5 cm (7 in) long were added to extend over the rim. Fewer few foliage, to hide the mechanics, and the six sprays of *Alchemilla mollis* with its tiny star-shaped flowers, were inserted between the centre stem and the outer rim. The remaining chrysanthemum flowers were added to complete the arrangement (see the photograph below) which was placed on a low stool in a dark corner.

Step 3

Step 4

Step 5

Finish

Summer sunshine

Height 43 cm (17 in)

Arranging flowers in a basket is not difficult. After all, it is just another container made of a different material; and you may use a basket with or without a handle. It can be arranged in any of the traditional shapes. The one in the photograph (below), is a symmetrical triangle.

A wet foam round on a foam saucer was held in place by a stub wire which had been passed through the foam and twisted around the handle of the basket at both sides.

Components
Basket 30.5 cm (12 in) long × 25.5 cm (10 in) wide × 5 cm (2 in) deep
Handle 25.5 cm (10 in) high
Foam saucer with wet plastic foam

Foliage
5 bushy sprays of *Lonicera* 'Baggesens Gold'
1 × 35.5 cm (14 in) for first placement at centre
2 × 18 cm (7 in) for either end, placement 2 & 3
2 × 15 cm (6 in) for the sides (by handle)
5 single pieces × 18 cm (7 in) for placing between the large leaves
5 honesty leaves for covering foam

5 rose leaves as foil for flowers and to cover stems

Flowers
4 sprays of carnations
1 × 28 cm (11 in) for No. 1 placement – 2 buds (open flowers removed)
2 × 24 cm (9½ in) for Nos. 2 and 3 placement – 2 buds (open flowers removed)
1 spray divided plus flowers from the other sprays = 10 flowers
9 roses
1 × 25.5 cm (10 in) for centre
5 × 16.5 cm (6½ in)
3 × 12.5 cm (5 in), recessed

Step 1

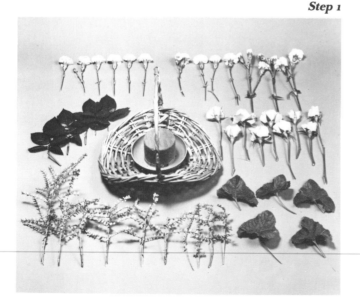

Step 2

Placement No. 1: a spray of *Lonicera*, 35.5 cm (14 in) long was inserted in the centre of the foam round in front of the handle. Two sprays 18 cm (7 in) long were placed one at either end.

Placement 2 and 3: two sprays of *Lonicera*, on either side by the handle, facing the front. Five *Lonicera* sprays 18 cm (7 in) long, were used to place between the larger leaves, and at the centre. Honesty leaves and rose foliage hid the mechanics and bare stems.

Spray carnations followed the 1, 2 and 3 outline placements

with the roses coming between. Three larger roses were recessed at the centre of the design.

The basket was placed on the hall table. It was raised on a wooden base 15 cm (6 in) × 10 cm (4 in) to give 2.5 cm (1 in) clearance, which allowed the flowers space to fall naturally over the edge.

Step 3

Step 4

Step 5

Finish

A discarded glass cake dish painted black was used for this informal grouping of roses.

The mechanics were a round of wet foam on a foam holder, fixed to the cake dish with adhesive. The longest stem, with two roses and one bud, was inserted in the centre of the foam. The three shorter flower stems were added to the centre, right and left. Five large rose leaves were placed at the base for balance, and to help hide the foam. Six rose blooms 12.5 cm (5 in) long

A gift of roses

Height 44.5 cm (17½ in)

Components
Glass cake dish on aluminium stand 6.5 cm (2½ in) high × 23 cm (9 in) diameter
Foam round

Foliage
5 large rose leaves
6 stems of rose foliage – 3 × 23 cm (9 in), 3 × 20 cm (8 in)

Flowers
4 stems of roses in flower and bud –
1 stem of 2 roses and 1 bud at 38 cm (15 in)
3 stems in tight bud at 35.5 cm (14 in)
9 roses – 7 × 12.5 cm (5 in), 2 × 15 cm (6 in)

Step 1

Step 2

were also arranged at this level. Three stems of foliage were placed to the back, and three stems to the front. The larger rose blooms were used for the middle of the design, the largest being recessed in the centre.

The arrangement seemed to lack sparkle, however; a contrast was needed, and the arrangement was lightened by being placed next to a blue ceramic cat.

Step 3

Step 4

Step 5

Finish

Dinner table harmony

Height 19 cm (7½ in)
Width 18 cm (7 in)
Length 56 cm (22 in)

Components
Sauce dish from dinner
service 23 cm (9 in) × 9 cm
(3½ in) × 9 cm (3½ in)
high
Wet foam 10 cm (4 in) × 6.5
cm (2½ in) × 11.5 cm (4½
in) high

Foliage
14 pieces of golden privet
2 × 24 cm
(9½ in)   } for each
4 × 19 cm   end of
(7½ in)   arrangement

4 × 10 cm (4 in) for front
and back
4 × 12.5 cm (6 in) for
continuation through design
6 *Mahonia* leaves
2 × 19 cm
(7½ in)   } transitional
4 × 12.5 cm   material
(5 in)

Flowers
10 gaillardias
2 small blooms 20 cm (8 in)
2 medium blooms 15 cm (6 in)
6 large blooms 12.5 cm
(5 in) for centre of
arrangement

The gaillardias and golden privet were chosen for their colour harmony with the dinner service.

The narrow rectangular sauce dish was chosen for its size and suitability for use with a refectory-type table which measured 194 cm (6 ft 6 in) × 84 cm (2 ft 9 in). The two longest pieces of privet, 24 cm (9½ in) long, were inserted at each end of wet foam which was 2.5 cm (1 in) above the rim of the dish. The four 19 cm (7½ in) pieces of privet, two at each end, were used to strengthen the outline shape, while the four 10 cm (4 in) pieces were added, two at the back of the arrangement and two in the front, to fall over the rim.

Step 1

Step 2

The two *Mahonia* leaves, each 19 cm (7½ in) long, were added at either end and the four shorter ones placed in the top of the foam, to radiate from the centre. The four smaller gaillardia flowers followed the line of the No. 1 placements. The six larger flowers, 12.5 cm (5 in) long, were inserted, one at each corner of the wet foam, to fall over the edge of the container, with the two remaining flowers in the centre. Finally, the four stems of outline foliage were placed between the centre flowers (see below).

Step 3

Step 4

Step 5

Finish

Fortunately, the stone wine bottle had a very small opening, so all the plant material fitted without the use of a wedge. Before starting the arrangement the bottle was filled with water.

Two pieces of dried honeysuckle stems were formed into circular shapes and tied together (see below). The large rose was placed in the centre, to the front, and the *Mahonia* leaf to the side, to give balance. (After inserting in the bottle neck, it may be necessary to adjust the angle of some of the plant material.)

As the bottle was long and narrow and the loops of honeysuckle relatively large, a base was necessary for balance. This was achieved by placing it slightly off-centre, on an upturned cheese board, measuring 20 cm (8 in) × 30.5 cm (12 in).

Single beauty

Height 66 cm (26 in)

Components
Stone wine bottle 29 cm
(11½ in) high

Foliage
1 large glycerined *Mahonia bealei* leaf
2 pieces dried honeysuckle, tied together in circles

Flowers
1 large pink or apricot coloured rose

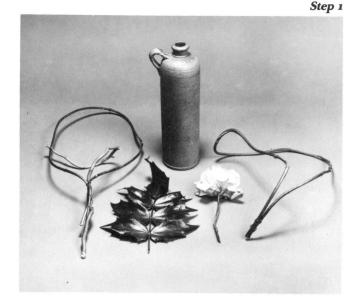

Step 1

Finish

This is a design which shows the beauty of these tall elegant gladioli flowers and the foliage which so closely protects them

The 6.5 cm (2½ in) pinholder was placed in the centre of the oval dish containing water. The flowers, with thin foliage attached, were arranged so that the tallest, 66 cm (26 in) long, was in the centre with the two others, 61 cm (24 in) and 47 cm (18½ in) long, at either side. The stems, 46 cm (18 in) and 40.5

cm (16 in) long, were placed to the centre front. The extra leaves were added at the back of the design to exclude the view of the fireplace.

The piece of driftwood gave visual weight at the base and hid the mechanics.

The finished arrangement was placed directly on to the hearth.

Fireplace interest

Height 66 cm (26 in)

Components
Shallow oval glass dish 5 cm (2 in) deep × 30 cm (12 in) long × 23 cm (9 in) wide
Piece of driftwood
6.5 cm (2½ in) pinholder

Foliage
3 separate gladioli leaves (the result of cutting flower stems shorter)
1 × 51 cm (20 in), 1 × 42 cm (16½ in), 1 × 30.5 cm (12 in)

Flowers
5 gladioli with their leaves attached
1 × 66 cm (26 in), 1 × 61 cm (24 in), 1 × 47 cm (18½ in), 1 × 46 cm (18 in), 1 × 40.5 cm (16 in)

Step 1

Finish

A stemmed container was necessary for this 'lazy S' design, so a grey ceramic cherub figurine container was chosen, in which was fixed a round of wet foam. The variegated *Weigela*, with its autumn colours of greeny silver and pinky bronze, made a perfect foil for the salmon coloured dahlias and the container.

The longest piece of curving *Weigela*, 38 cm (15 in), was inserted in the foam so that its tip was directly over the centre of the foam. Two more pieces, 33 cm (13 in) and 28 cm (11 in) long, were placed to the left, the shortest piece being the lowest (see below). The No. 2 placement of *Weigela*, 21.5 cm (8½

Autumn glory

Height 61 cm (24 in)

Components
Grey-stemmed ceramic
container 23 cm (9 in) high
Wet foam on foam anchor

Foliage
12 pieces *Weigela florida*
'Variegata'
3 pieces: 1 × 38 cm (15 in),
1 × 33 cm (13 in), 1 × 28
cm (11 in) for *top curve*
3 pieces: 1 × 21.5 cm (8½
in), 1 × 16.5 cm (6½ in), 1
× 11.5 cm (4½ in) for *lower
curve*
6 pieces: 6 × 10 cm (4 in) for
centre

Flowers
6 dahlias
2 flowers: 1 × 34 cm (13½
in), 1 × 25.5 cm (10 in) for
top curve
2 flowers: 1 × 20 cm (8 in),
1 × 16.5 cm (6½ in) for
lower curve
2 flowers: 1 × 15 cm (6 in),
1 × 10 cm (4 in) for *centre*

Step 1

Step 2

in) long, was placed in the side of the foam to fall over and curve downwards over the rim of the container, thus completing the 'O' shape. The line was strengthened by the addition of two more pieces, 16.5 cm (6½ in) and 11.5 cm (4½ in), to the right side, the shorter piece being closer to the centre.

The six remaining stems of foliage were used to create the centre of interest and hide the foam. Two pieces follow the No. 1 and 2 placements; the first one in front of No. 1, and the second over the No. 2 placement, falling in the same direction, to hide the foam. The remaining foliage pieces were placed two to the

front and two to the back, hiding the remainder of the foam. Four small flowers followed the outline. At No. 1 placement the flowers are 34 cm (13½ in) and 25.5 cm (10 in) long, and at No. 2 large flowers are placed at the centre of interest, one 15 cm (6 in); the shorter one, 10 cm (4 in) long, is recessed.

This is a suitable arrangement for limited space. It was designed for the corner of a desk, and was placed on a grey-green velvet base, 18 cm (7 in) diameter.

Step 3

Step 4

Step 5

Finish

Before the fall

Height 51 cm (20 in)

Before the leaves fall forsythia, having provided us in springtime with sprays of lovely yellow flowers, gives us beautifully tinted brown and yellow-green foliage. Because of its plentiful growth and colour, it was used without the introduction of larger leaves. Combined with the velvet-like rudbeckia flowers the finished design exuded rich glowing harmony.

It was designed for a polished wood base, 38 cm (15 in) × 20 cm (8 in) × 2.5 cm (1 in) deep, and arranged in wet foam in a foam dish. As the left side of the arrangement is the shorter, the dish was placed to the left, off centre. The No. 1 placement had

Components
Foam dish with wet foam

Foliage
10 pieces of forsythia
for placement No. 1
2 pieces: 1 × 43 cm (17 in), 1 × 28 cm (11 in)
for placement No. 2
1 piece: 1 × 18 cm (7 in)
for placement No. 3
1 piece: 1 × 33 cm (13 in)
for placements Nos. 4 & 5
2 pieces: 2 × 15 cm (6 in)
For centre   4 pieces: 4 × 15 cm (6 in)

Flowers
16 rudbeckia
1 × 38 cm (15 in), 1 × 35.5 cm (14 in), 1 × 30.5 cm (12 in), 5 × 25.5 cm (10 in), 6 × 15 cm (6 in), 1 × 18 cm (7 in), 1 × 16.5 cm (6½ in)

Step 1

Step 2

two pieces of foliage, one 43 cm (17 in) long and one 28 cm (11 in) long, to hide the lower bare stem of No. 1. At the No. 2 placement a 18 cm (7 in) stem was inserted, and at placement No. 3 a 33 cm (13 in) stem was placed. At placements Nos. 4 and 5 both stems were 15 cm (6 in). This completed the boundaries of the arrangement.

The remaining four pieces, each 15 cm (6 in) long, were included to fill the centre and the back. The flowers followed the foliage placements, the smaller ones to the outer edges and three large ones being reserved for the centre of interest. The flower at

30.5 cm (12 in) came on the No. 1 placement line; the one at 18 cm (7 in) was in the centre, forward over rim; and the one at 16.5 cm (6½ in) recessed in the centre of interest.

The completed arrangement was placed on a wide, low shelf by a window to catch the autumn sunshine.

Step 3

Step 4

Step 5

Finish

Of the nine chrysanthemum leaves taken from the two flower sprays, four were placed around the candle in the centre to hide the wet foam, and the remaining five at regular intervals around the rim, between the five 12.5 cm (5 in) long *Alstroemeria* flowers. Five chrysanthemums, 10 cm (4 in) long, were placed above the chrysanthemum leaves.

All the other smaller flowers, four chrysanthemums of 7.5 cm

Twilight

Height 44.5 cm (17½ in)

Components
Candlestick of
brown
wood and
copper
24 cm (9½ in)
high

Candle cup with wet foam
Candle 20 cm (8 in) long

Foliage
9 chrysanthemum leaves to
hide mechanics
8 pieces of *Hypericum* with
berries to match wood of
candlestick
2 × 12.5 cm (5 in), 6 × 10
cm (4 in)

Flowers
2 sprays of yellow
Alstroemeria which provide
5 × 12.5 cm (5 in) flowers
with buds attached
5 *Alstroemeria* flowers 5 ×
10 cm (4 in)
2 sprays of chrysanthemums
(to match colouring of
candlestick) with: 5 blooms
× 10 cm (4 in), 4 blooms ×
7.5 cm (3 in)

Step 1

Step 2

(3 in) and seven *Alstroemeria* of 10 cm (4 in), were inserted between the candle and the outer placements. Eight hypericum berried stems were included, two of 12.5 cm (5 in) to the front and back of the candle and six of 10 cm (4 in) at intervals between the flowers.

The design was placed in the centre of a supper table.

Step 3

Step 4

Step 5

Finish

In the autumn sunshine, *Cotoneaster franchettii*, with its leaves and rich harvest of red berries, is a joy to behold. The first time I became aware of the beauty of this shrub was when seeing it arranged in a white container.

The longest stem, 48 cm (19 in) long in this arrangement, was placed in the centre of the vase and was held in position by a cut end of the 4 cm (1½ in) gauge wire netting used as mechanics. The four 33 cm (13 in) pieces of angular growth were arranged to the side and front so as to fall naturally over the rim of the vase. The four remaining straight sprays were placed between this

Contrast

Height 48 cm (19 in)

Components
White vase 25.5 cm (10 in)
high × 7.5 cm (3 in)
diameter at top
Crumpled wire netting –
4 cm (1½ in) gauge

Foliage
9 pieces of red-berried
Cotoneaster
1 × 48 cm (19 in)
4 (angular growth) × 33 cm
(13 in)
4 (straight sprays): 1 × 46
cm (18 in), 1 × 28 cm (11
in), 1 × 20 cm (8 in), 1 × 18
cm (7 in)

Flowers
6 chrysanthemums
3 smaller outline flowers: 1
× 40.5 cm (16 in), 1 × 38
cm (15 in), 1 × 35.5 cm (14
in)
3 large centre flowers: 1 ×
25.5 (10 in), 1 × 23 cm (9
in), 1 × 20 cm (8 in)

Step 1

Step 2

outline, closer together in the centre for a concentration of colour and to hide the wire. The six white single chrysanthemum flowers were added, the longer to the outside and the shorter towards the centre. When using wire netting there is a certain amount of movement of the plant material, but this can be adjusted as a final step.

The finished arrangement was placed on a dark cork mat, 16.5 cm (6½ in) × 16.5 cm (6½ in), on the wooden shelf of a room divider.

Step 3

Step 4

Step 5

Finish

Fruit and flowers

Height 47 cm (18½ in)

When flowers are scarce, fruit and gourds may be used as a colourful substitute.

In this arrangement, a heavy foam holder was used to hold the wet foam. This gave stability and made the construction of the design easier. The longest stem of *Kniphofia* was used as the No. 1 placement. The No. 2 placement was an 18 cm (7 in) stemmed *Bergenia* leaf, and No. 3 placement was a 20 cm (8 in) stemmed *Bergenia* leaf. The four small 5 cm (2 in) leaves were tucked in low at the back and sides to cover the foam.

Four more leaves were added; a 25.5 cm (10 in) stem behind,

Components
Wicker tray 30.5 cm (12 in) diameter
Foam saucer with wet foam on a metal holder
Cocktail sticks

Foliage
10 *Bergenia* leaves with stems
1 × 25.5 cm (10 in), 1 × 23 cm (9 in), 1 × 20 cm (8 in), 1 × 16.5 cm (6½ in), 2 × 18 cm (7 in), 4 × 5 cm (2 in)

Flowers
3 *Kniphofia* flowers

1 × 43 cm (17 in), 1 × 33 cm (13 in), 1 × 28 cm (11 in)

Fruit
3 apples about 5 cm (2 in) diameter
3 gourds
1 × about 7.5 cm (3 in) diameter, 1 × 6.5 cm (2½ in) diameter, pear shaped, 1 × 4 cm (1½ in) diameter, round
1 tangerine of 6 cm (2¼ in) diameter

Step 1

Step 2

and one of 23 cm (9 in) to the left of No. 1 placement. A 16.5 cm (6½ in) leaf was placed in the centre to hide the stem of *Kniphofia* and, to the right, one of 18 cm (7 in), between placements 1 and 3. The remaining two *Kniphofia* flowers, 33 cm (13 in) and 28 cm (11 in), were added in the centre, in line with the first flower. The largest gourd was placed on the tray to the left-hand side. The three small apples mounted on cocktail sticks, were attached to the foam, the left-hand apple resting on the gourd (see photograph below). The remaining two gourds were placed towards centre right, with the tangerine mounted on a cocktail stick

pushed into foam and resting on the pear-shaped gourd. A piece of plasticine or similar material will hold the gourds in position.

This interesting design gave a splash of colour to an otherwise dark hall.

Step 3

Step 4

Step 5

Finish

Two leafless branches of beech picked up on a walk were the inspiration for this arrangement.

They were impaled in a 6.5 cm (2½ in) pinholder inside a food tin containing water. The branches were placed to form an almost enclosed space. The two stems of pernettia berries were placed immediately in front, one on either side, the lighter

An autumn walk

Height 61 cm (24 in)

Components
Oval wood slice 28 cm (11 in) × 18 cm (7 in) at widest part
Pinholder 6.5 cm (2½ in) diameter
Food tin 7.5 cm (3 in) diameter × 4 cm (1½ in) high
Silver birch bark

Foliage
2 bare branches of beech
1 × 46 cm (18 in), 1 × 43 cm (17 in)

2 honesty leaves
1 × 10 cm (4 in), 1 × 12.5 cm (5 in)
2 sprays of pernettya
1 × 23 cm (9 in), 1 × 18 cm (7 in) with dark and light berries

Flowers
3 anemones
2 cerise
1 × 16.5 cm (6½ in), 1 × 12.5 cm (5 in)
1 blue × 10 cm (4 in)

Step 1

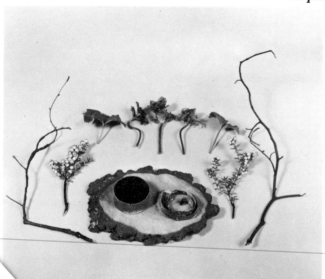

Step 2

coloured branch to the right, and the darker one on the left. Two honesty leaves were added – one facing forward and the other facing backwards. The design was completed by the addition of the three anemone flowers (see photograph below). The silver birch bark hid the food tin.

This arrangement was enjoyed on the kitchen window sill.

Step 3

Step 4

Step 5

Finish

From the shrub garden

An arrangement of foliage can provide an area of restful beauty. It is essential to have a number of different varieties, so as to vary the colour, form and texture. In this design there are eight different varieties to balance the heavy pottery container. Usually four or five varieties are sufficient.

Placement No. 1 was made up of the largest *Mahonia* leaf, strengthened and balanced at the back by the addition of the *Aucuba* leaf, 1 *Senecio* spray 25.5 cm (10 in) long and a *Mahonia* leaf 20 cm (8 in) long. Placements 2 and 3 were of *Senecio* sprays, 15

Height 61 cm (24 in)

Components
Pottery jar with candlecup on top 25.5 cm (10 in) high
Red felt-covered base 11.5 cm (4½ in) diameter
Wet foam

Foliage
4 large *Mahonia* leaves
1 × 38 cm (15 in), 3 × 20 cm (8 in)
8 *Senecio laxifolius* sprays
1 × 25.5 cm (10 in), 2 × 23 cm (9 in), 2 × 15 cm (6 in), 3 × 20 cm (8 in)
1 *Aucuba* leaf – 1 × 20 cm (8 in)

Garrya elliptica 2 × 21.5 cm (8½ in)
3 *Bergenia* leaves
1 × 16.5 cm (6½ in), 2 × 18 cm (7 in)
5 pieces of thuja 'Rheingold'
2 × 21.5 cm (8½ in), 1 × 18 cm (7 in), 2 × 15 cm (6 in)
3 stems of *Euonymus*
1 × 25.5 cm (10 in), 1 × 18 cm (7 in), 1 × 12.5 cm (5 in)
2 ivy sprays 2 × 18 cm (7 in)

Fruit
7 stems *Arbutus unedo* fruit (strawberry tree)

Step 1

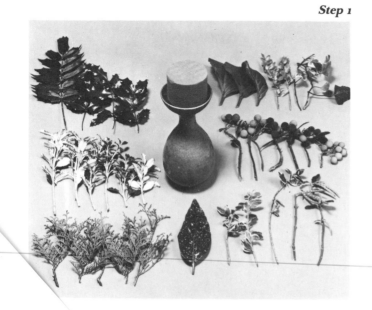

Step 2

cm (6 in) long, and placements 6 and 7 were of *Senecio* sprays 23 cm (9 in) long and the remaining two *Mahonia* leaves, 20 cm (8 in) long. The tasseled 21.5 cm (8½ in) stems of *Garrya elliptica*, used for variation, were added in the area of placement 7, to the right of No. 1 stem. For the centre of interest the three *Bergenia* leaves were used. One at 16.5 cm (6½ in) was placed at the base of No. 1 placement and the other two, 18 cm (7 in) long, placed at either side. The fine bronzy feathery foliage of thuja was inserted with two stems of 15 cm (6 in) at placements 2 and 3, two stems of 21.5 cm (8½ in) at placements 6 and 7, one stem of 18 cm (7 in) in the centre, with its sprays falling to the left and

right, over the rim of the container. The centre of interest was highlighted by three stems, 25.5 cm (10 in), 18 cm (7 in) and 12.5 cm (5 in) long of *Euonymus* and two 18 cm (7 in) variegated ivy stems. The three remaining sprays of *Senecio* were inserted at the back for added balance. As a final touch, seven stems of *Arbutus unedo* fruits (strawberry tree) were placed through the design. The arrangement was placed on a red felt base, 11.5 cm (4½ in) diameter, towards the back of a sideboard. The base accentuated the colour of the overall design.

Step 3

Step 4

Step 5

Finish

A matt blue, unglazed cereal bowl was used. Two stems, 28 cm (11 in) long, of prostrate juniper were inserted in the wet foam to form an inverted crescent. Two stems, 15 cm (6 in) long, were added to strengthen the line. For the centre, four variegated ivy leaves were placed so as to hide the foam and to give a focal point. Three flowers were added at each side to the crescent outline, the longest one at 23 cm (9 in) with two at 18 cm (7 in) to the right and left of the 23 cm (9 in) flowers.

Coffee morning

Height 30 cm (12 in)

Components
Cereal bowl (matt blue)
Wet foam on foam holder

Foliage
9 pieces of juniper foliage
2 × 28 cm (11 in), 2 × 15 cm (6 in), 2 × 10 cm (4 in), 3 × 11.5 cm (4½ in)
4 variegated ivy leaves × 5 cm (2 in)

Flowers
10 anemones, assorted colours
2 × 23 cm (9 in) for sides
4 × 18 cm (7 in) for sides
2 × 5 cm (2 in) for hanging over brim
2 × 2.5 cm (1 in) for centre of interest

Step 1

Step 2

The remaining four flowers were used for the centre, one at 5 cm (2 in) looking towards the back and falling over the rim, and another at 5 cm (2 in) following the same pattern over the front. The other two flowers, 2.5 cm (1 in) long, were recessed in the centre. Looking down into the arrangement it should be a definite crescent shape, lower in the centre than at the ends.

The anemones were chosen to repeat the colour of the ceramic coffee cups.

Step 3

Step 4

Step 5

Finish

Growing plants and flowers

Height 61 cm (24 in)

A brown pottery bowl, decorated with cream patterns, was used. About two handfuls of washed gravel (for drainage) with four pieces of bonfire charcoal (to keep components pure) were placed in the bottom of the bowl. This was covered by a layer of John Innes no. 2 compost, and the base was then ready for the plants to be put into position. All plants were removed from their pots before placing in the bowl.

The *Ficus pumila*, 61 cm (24 in) tall, was placed in the centre of the bowl at the back. To the left-hand side, the *Begonia metallica* was placed sideways so that its foliage flowed over the rim of the

Components
Bowl 28 cm (11 in) diameter
× 15 cm (6 in) deep
Food tin with wet foam
About 2 handfuls of washed gravel
3 or 4 pieces of charcoal
(2 lb) bag of John Innes compost no. 2

House Plants
Ficus pumila 61 cm (24 in) tall in 10 cm (4 in) pot

Solanum capsicastrum 40.5 cm (16 in) tall in 9 cm (3½ in) pot
Begonia metallica 20 cm (8 in) tall in 9 cm (3½ in) pot
Hedera (ivy) 15 cm (6 in) tall with 3 sprays – 30.5 cm (12 in), 33 cm (13 in) and 35.5 cm (14 in) long in 9 cm (3½ in) pot
4 chrysanthemum sprays

Step 1

Step 2

bowl. To hold the plants in position, compost was added. To the right-hand side the berried *Solanum capsicastrum* was added in an upright position to give more bulk to the centre.

The food tin, filled with wet foam for the cut flowers, was added, slightly to the left and in front of the *Ficus pumila* (see photograph below). The *Hedera* 'Glacier' (ivy) was placed to the right, and in front, so that its trails fell over the front of the bowl. More compost was added to hold all the components in place. Lastly, the four sprays of chrysanthemum were arranged in the container to give the centre colour and interest.

The arrangement makes a long-lasting, easy to maintain design. Remember that the plants require watering. The colour scheme may also be changed, since fresh flowers can be added when necessary.

Step 3

Step 4

Step 5

Finish

The materials for this arrangement are large and bulky, so a metal holder was used to hold the wet foam in position. More than one cocktail stick may be necessary to hold a heavy fruit in the foam, and sometimes a longer one is needed. Two can be spliced together with adhesive tape.

The first placement is made using the four pieces of New Zealand flax, and the four large *Mahonia* leaves are inserted at the base (see photograph, below), together with the two bunches of grapes. Cocktail sticks were first taped to the stems of

Festive buffet

Height 40.5 cm (16 in)

Components
Glass cake stand 23 cm (9 in) diameter × 7.5 cm (3 in) high
Wet foam on metal holder to give weight

Foliage
4 pieces New Zealand flax 'dazzler', 30.5 cm (12 in) long
7 *Mahonia* leaves (red colour)
4 large leaves × 18 cm (7 in) (winter colouring: red/green)

3 small leaves × 10 cm (4 in)

Fruit
2 deep red apples about 21.5 cm (8½ in) circumference
3 tangerines
2 bunches grapes, one red and one green
2 large pears
5 cox apples, various sizes

Step 1

Step 2

the grape bunches to give extra support. The design was then built up by placing the heavier fruit at the bottom. The smaller fruit, while being attached to the wet foam with cocktail sticks, may sometimes rest on the larger pieces. Colour interest was maintained through the arrangement.

The shorter *Mahonia* leaves were added to help with recession and divide up the larger shapes. Time taken experimenting with the placing of fruit is not wasted. As this is for front view only, less colourful apples were added to the back to give balance and stability. A pineapple could have been used at the top but sometimes they are difficult to obtain in the right size.

This colourful arrangement could have a two-fold purpose; to be used as decoration only, or to be eaten as a dessert!

Step 3

Step 4

Step 5

Finish

The Japanese tea-pot chosen for this arrangement was part filled with broken foam. The wedge of wet foam, extending above the pot, was resting on this layer of broken foam.

Nine sprays of jasmine and nine libertia leaves, all of the same lengths, 1 of 32 cm (12½ in), 1 of 28 cm (11 in), 1 of 20 cm (8 in), 3 of 18 cm (7 in), and 3 of 14 cm (5½ in), form the outline (see photograph, below). The five variegated geranium leaves were placed in the centre to add extra interest, and served the useful purpose of hiding the foam. Four of the longest chrysanthemums were placed to follow the outlines of libertia and jasmine, and the five larger flowers at 11.5 cm (4½ in) long, and the remaining 4 of 12.5 cm (5 in) sprays of jasmine, were added to the centre. As the libertia leaves were available, they were chosen to relate to the leaf pattern on the tea-pot. However, any small-leaved shrub could have been used, for instance, escallonia, privet, etc.

The arrangement was a cheerful greeting for the winter breakfast table.

Brightness for breakfast

Height 40.5 cm (16 in)

Components
Japanese tea-pot with bamboo handle, overall height 21.5 cm (8½ in)
Wet foam

Foliage
9 libertia leaves
1 × 32 cm (12½ in), 1 × 28 cm (11 in), 1 × 20 cm (8 in), 3 × 18 cm (7 in), 3 × 14 cm (5½ in)
5 variegated houseplant geranium leaves × 11.5 cm (4½ in)

Flowers
13 sprays of winter jasmine
9 × same lengths as libertia
4 × 12.5 cm (5 in)
3 sprays of yellow flowered chrysanthemum (9 flowers)
1 × 19 cm (7½ in), 3 × 15 cm (6 in), 5 × 11.5 cm (4½ in)

Suggested plants to use

It is surprising how much can be grown in a small space, even without a garden. A tub or window box can produce a useful amount of foliage, and the modern growing bag has great possibilities. A garden, if large enough, can provide both flowers and shrubs, but with limited space foliage is more important. A background of leaves adds interest to an arrangement and reduces the number of blooms required. Flowers can always be bought, but although florists have some foliage at times, the choice is usually not great.

Try to grow the more interesting varieties of a plant. For example, with *Ligustrum* (privet) choose the variety *aureomarginatum* (golden privet), which has a wide irregular border and is delightful in all types of arrangements. It is an evergreen, and so it can be used all the year round.

Grow the same plant in different situations for variation in colour and growth rate. In a warmer spot a plant may mature more quickly and give material earlier, thus increasing the usefulness by extending the cutting time. *Mahonia aquifolium* treated in this way produces interesting foliage of different colours: reds, greens and browns. The one I grow that is exposed to southwesterly winds is a beautiful red, while the others remain a green and brown.

Growing ground covering plants eliminates the amount of weeding you must do and provides useful flower material; for example periwinkle and ivy are suitable for planting beneath the taller shrubs, with the added advantage of making maximum use of the available planting area.

The following lists of foliage and flowers may help in the selection of suitable plant material for use through the different seasons of the year. You may find the same plant listed under more than one heading e.g. *Macleaya cordata* (plume poppy), the leaf of which is used as a centre of interest, while the flowering stem may be used as outline material.

These plants may either be obtained from garden centres or, in many cases, grown at home.
* plants used in the photographic section
T trees

Outline material	Colour	Season
*T *Alnus aurea* (alder)	pink stems with pale yellow leaves	spring, summer
* Alstroemeria	yellow, pink or white flowers	all the year
Aquilegia	red and white, or mauve and green flowers	early summer
Artemisia ludoviciana	silver-grey feathery foliage	summer, autumn
Aruncus sylvester	small, feathery white flowers	summer
Aster (michaelmas daisy)	white, blue or pink flowers	autumn
Astilbe	white, pink or red flowers	mid-summer
Berberis thunbergii	dark-red, small leaves	summer, autumn

Outline material	Colour	Season	Outline material	Colour	Season
* Carnation (spray)	white, yellow, orange, red or pink flowers	all the year	Hedera 'Gold Heart' (ivy)	small green leaves with gold splashes	all the year
* Chrysanthe-mum (spray)	various colours of flowers	all the year	* Hypericum elatum 'Elstead'	yellow flowers salmon-red berries	summer autumn, winter
T Corylus avellana 'Contorta' (hazel)	light green stems	winter (use without leaves)	T Ilex aquifolium (holly) J. C. van Tol	dark, shiny green leaves with red berries	all the year (esp. christmas season)
* Cotoneaster franchettii	grey-green leaves pink flowers orange-red berries	all the year summer winter	T Ilex aquifolium (holly) 'Bacciflava'	green leaves yellow berries	all the year christmas season
* Delphinium	blue, white or pink flowers	summer, autumn	* Iris	green sword-like leaves, flowers of various colours	spring, autumn
Elaeagnus pungens 'Variegata'	green leaves with yellow edges	all the year	* Jasminum nudiflorum	small yellow flowers small green leaves	winter, spring summer
* Escallonia	green leaves small pink flowers	all the year summer	* Juniper horizontalis	blue-green feathery foliage	all the year
* Euonymus japonica 'aureo-picta'	green leaves with yellow splashes	all the year	* Kniphofia	long-stemmed, poker-shaped flower heads in shades of orange	summer, autumn
* Euonymus 'Silver Queen'	green leaves with white edges	all the year	Larkspur	blue, pink or white flowers	summer
* Ferns (common)	green fronds	spring, late autumn	* Lathyrus latifolius (everlasting) sweet pea)	white and mauve flowers green leaves	summer all the year
* Forsythia	sprays of yellow flowers green foliage	spring summer, autumn	* Libertia	green, narrow strap-like leaves	all the year
* Garrya elliptica	grey-green tassels	winter, spring	* Ligustrum aureo-marginatum (privet)	green leaves with gold border	all the year
* Gladiolus	green leaves and variety of flower colours	summer, autumn			
* Hedera 'Glacier' (ivy)	small green leaves with white edges	all the year			

Outline material	Colour	Season	Outline material	Colour	Season
Lonicera caprifolium (cottage garden variety)	green leaves cream flowers	all the year summer	Roses (floribunda and climbing)	flowers of various colours	summer, autumn
Lonicera japonica	yellow and green leaves	all the year	T *Salix matsudana* 'Tortuosa' (willow)	light green leaves white silky buds greeny yellow bare stems	summer, autumn spring winter
* *Lonicera nitida* 'Baggesen's Gold' (honeysuckle)	tiny, gold leaves	summer, autumn	* *Senecio laxifolius*	small grey-green leaves	all the year
Lupin	yellow, pink or mauve flowers	summer	Sidalcea	pink or white flowers	summer
Macleaya cordata	buff flowers	summer	T *Sorbus aria* 'Lutescens' (white beam)	whitish leaves	spring
Montbretia	red and orange flowers	autumn	Vinca	green-white leaves	all the year
Nepeta (cat mint)	blue flowers	summer	* *Weigela florida* 'Variegata'	pale green sprays of cream-edged leaves pink flowers	spring to autumn summer
* Pernettya	small, hard green leaves pink-purple berries	all the year autumn, winter			
* *Phormium tenax* (New Zealand flax)	large, sword-like leaves either green-red or cream	all the year			
Pittosporum	small green or silver leaves	all the year			
Polystichum aculeatum	green pinnate fronds	spring, late autumn			
T* *Prunus pissardii*	sprays of pink blossom brown leaves bare branches	spring summer, autumn winter			
Rosa rubrifolia	blue-grey foliage	spring, summer autumn			

Transitional material	Colour	Season	Transitional material	Colour	Season
Achillea	yellow flower	summer, autumn	*Hosta undulata*	small green leaves	late spring to autumn
Alchemilla mollis (lady's mantle)	acid-green leaves and small yellow flowers	summer, early autumn	*Hosta undulata* 'Variegata'	shiny green leaves with central white splash	late spring to autumn
Anemone japonica	pink-white flowers	late summer	* *Lunaria* (honesty)	green leaves, slightly metallic appearance	all the year
Aster	pink and blue flowers	autumn	* *Mahonia aquifolium*	green pinnate leaves, sometimes turning red	all the year
Astrantia major	white and pink flowers	summer	* *Mahonia bealei*	large leaves	all the year
T *Chamaecyparis obtusa*	golden feathery leaves	all the year	*Nerine bowdenii*	pink flowers	late autumn
Choisya ternata (Mexican orange blossom)	dark green leaves white flowers	all the year summer	Phlox	pink, white or red flowers	summer
* *Chrysanthemum parthenium* (feverfew)	acid-green soft, deeply cut foliage	all the year	*Ruta graveolens* (rue)	blue-grey foliage	all the year
* Chrysanthe-mum (spray)	flowers, all colours	all the year	*Sedum spectabile*	pink or red flowers	autumn
* Daffodil	yellow flowers	spring	*Senecio maritima* 'Diamond'	silvery-white, indented leaves	summer, autumn
* Dahlia	green foliage and various coloured flowers	summer, autumn	*Senecio maritima* 'Silver Dust'	silvery-white, fine leaves	summer, autumn
Euphorbia griffithii	flame flowers	summer, autumn	*Skimmia japonica*	green leaves pointed clusters of cream flowers red berries	all the year late spring autumn
Euphorbia polychroma	yellow flowers	spring, summer	*Stachys lanata* (lamb's ears)	silky, grey, felt-like leaves	spring to autumn
* Ferns	fronds, various greens	summer, autumn	* *Tellima purpurea*	bronze leaves	all the year
* *Hedera canariensis* 'Variegata' (ivy)	leaves with dark green centre and silvery white-grey border	all the year	T Thuja 'Rheingold'	golden, yellow, feathery leaves with reddish tinges in autumn	all the year
			Viburnum opulus	greenish flower balls	summer
			* *Viburnum tinus* 'Laurustinus'	small green leaves pink flowers	all the year winter, spring

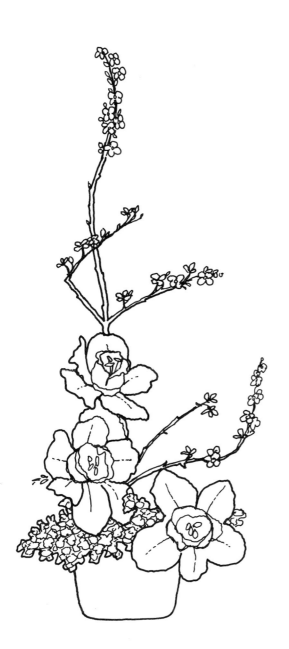

Centre or points of interest	Colour	Season
Aucuba japonica (spotted laurel)	pale green spotted leaves	all the year
Anthurium	red, pink or white flowers	all the year
* Apple	green, yellow or red fruit	all the year
T* *Arbutus unedo* (strawberry tree)	green leaves with cream flowers and red fruits	winter
Arum italicum 'Pictum'	green leaves with marbled-white veins	winter, spring
* *Bergenia cordifolia*	heart-shaped green leaves changing later to red shading	all the year
* *Bergenia crassifolia*	spoon-shaped green foliage	all the year
* Chrysanthemum	flowers of all colours	all the year
* Crocus	yellow, blue or white flowers	spring
* Dahlia	flowers of all colours	autumn
Digitalis (foxglove)	soft green leaves	all the year
Fatshedera	large ivy-shaped green leaves	all the year
* *Fatsia japonica*	rounded deeply cut, green leaves	all the year
* Geranium varieties	rounded green leaves, reds variegated, green and white	summer
* Gerbera	flowers, all colours	all the year
* Gaillardia	browny red, orange or flame flowers	summer, autumn

Centre or points of interest	Colour	Season
* Grape	green, white or black fruit	all the year
Hedera canariensis 'Variegata'	green leaves with large silver-grey markings	all the year
Helleborus orientalis, foetidus or *corsicus*	variously shaped foliage	summer, autumn
Hemerocallis	pink, orange or yellow flowers	summer
Hosta fortuneii 'Albopicta'	large yellow leaves with pale green edges	late spring to autumn
* *Hosta sieboldiana*	large blue-grey and veined leaves	late spring to autumn
* Iris	flowers of all colours	spring, summer
Iris foetidissima	orange seed heads	autumn, winter
Lemon	acid-yellow fruit	all the year
Lilium arum	white flowers	autumn
* Lilium 'Enchantment'	orange-pink flowers	all the year
Lilium longiflorum	white flowers	all the year
Macleaya cordata (plume poppy)	greyish green leaves	summer, autumn
Papaver orientalis (poppy)	red, pink or white flowers	late spring, summer
Peach	peach-coloured fruit	all the year
Pear	yellow-brown fruit	all the year

Centre or points of interest	Colour	Season
Peony	white, yellow or pink flowers	summer
* Roses	fllowers of all colours	summer, autumn
* Rudbeckia	orange flowers with brown centre	summer, autumn
Skimmia	rosettes of green leaves	all the year

Ideas bank

The illustrations which appear on the following four pages are included to sharpen your imagination. Copy the ideas by all means, but do also try to extend the principles that lie within them, to create your own variations and original designs. Remember – you are only limited in what you can do by your own imagination!

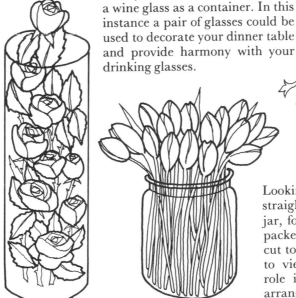

This arrangement gives the impression of being one set piece. It is, in fact, two separate arrangements in two identical wine glasses which, standing side by side, marry together harmoniously. Another glass might also be added, of course.

In this arrangement the solid colour of the plate is integral to the design. In this instance the white of the peonies and the green of the leaves contrast clearly with the red of the plate. Obviously, the same principles can be applied to plates of any solid colour.

It may not occur to you to think of a wine glass as a container. In this instance a pair of glasses could be used to decorate your dinner table and provide harmony with your drinking glasses.

There is no rule that says flowers have to appear outside of their container! A slim 'high-ball' glass has been used in this instance to contain miniature roses and their foliage.

Looking at glass again; here a straight-sided container, a honey jar, for instance, has been tightly packed with tulips. The stems, cut to the same length, are clearly to view and play an important role in the overall effect of the arrangement.

I have included some seasonal ideas which you might find inspirational at Easter and Christmas time. But do also bear in mind that similar arrangements can be created for the four seasons or any other festive occasion.

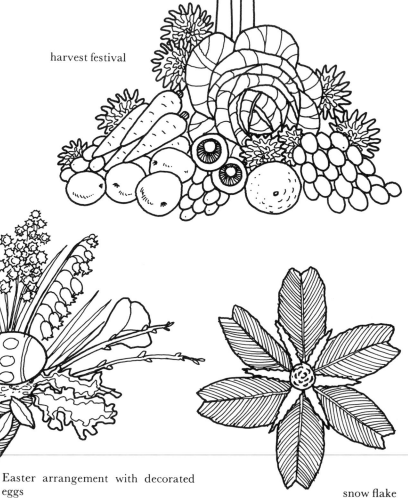

harvest festival

Easter arrangement with decorated eggs

snow flake

wreath

swag

1

2

3   Christmas tree arrangement

mistletoe ball

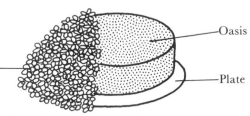

Cultivated daisies

Oasis

Plate

Why not re-vamp something and turn it into an acceptable container? Here I have pressed a coffee tin and biscuit box into service. Covered in glue then wrapped by thin rope, or even string, they change their character completely!

Here is a pretty and impressive arrangement which looks very good on a low coffee table. Use cultivated daisies or similarly petalled flowers – preferably of one colour. The stems are pushed into a circular oasis, so that when finished the flowers hide everything; including the plate upon which it all rests. Don't stand the oasis in water – water from the top as necessary.

Where you have a single, spectacular bloom, float it on water in a pretty glass bowl with a couple of leaves or a piece of fern to set it off.

Just an idea upon which to build. You may well have several objects around the house which can be co-opted into a flower arrangement. You do not always have to rely solely on the flowers alone.

When flowers are plentiful in the Summer, try arranging them as one colour posies in straight sided glasses of differing heights. Then arrange the glasses into a group to create this kind of effect.

Index

VISUAL INDEX

page 62

page 60

page 73

page 70

page 80

page 102

page 82

page 88

page 98

page 83

page 66

page 92

SUBJECT INDEX

Page numbers in italics refer to illustrations.